MOTHER-CHILD CONVERSATIONS ABOUT GENDER: UNDERSTANDING THE ACQUISITION OF ESSENTIALIST BELIEFS

Susan A. Gelman
Marianne G. Taylor
Simone P. Nguyen

WITH COMMENTARY BY
Campbell Leaper
Rebecca S. Bigler

Willis F. Overton
Series Editor

MONOGRAPHS OF THE SOCIETY FOR RESEARCH IN CHILD DEVELOPMENT

Serial No. 275, Vol. 69, No. 1, 2004

Blackwell Publishing

Boston, Massachusetts   Oxford, United Kingdom

Mother-Child Conversations about Gender

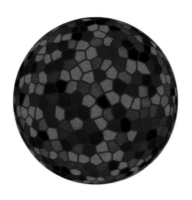

Susan A. Gelman
Marianne G. Taylor
Simone P. Nguyen

with commentary by

Campbell Leaper
Rebecca S. Bigler

MONOGRAPHS OF THE SOCIETY FOR RESEARCH IN CHILD DEVELOPMENT

Willis F. Overton, *Editor*

MOTHER-CHILD CONVERSATIONS ABOUT GENDER: UNDERSTANDING THE ACQUISITION OF ESSENTIALIST BELIEFS

CONTENTS

COMMENTARY

ABSTRACT

The present study examines mother–child conversations about gender, to examine (1) children's essentialist beliefs about gender, and (2) the role of maternal input in fostering such beliefs. We videotaped 72 mothers and their sons/daughters (mean ages 2.7, 4.7, or 6.7) discussing a picture book that depicted stereotypical and counter-stereotypical gendered activities (e.g., a boy playing football; a woman race-car driver). Mothers and children also completed measures of gender stereotyping and gender constancy. Results indicate more explicit endorsement of gender stereotypes among children than among mothers. Indeed, mothers provided little in the way of explicit stereotyped input. Nonetheless, mothers expressed gender concepts through a number of more implicit means, including reference to categories of gender (generics), labeling of gender, and contrasting males versus females. Gender-stereotype endorsement from children emerged early (by 2–1/2 years of age), but also underwent important developmental changes, most notably a rapid increase between 2 and 4 years of age in the focus on generic *categories* of gender. Variation in speech (across individuals and across contexts) cannot be characterized along a single dimension of degree of gender-typing; rather, there seemed to be differences in how focused a speaker was on gender (or not), with some speakers providing more talk about gender (both stereotyped and non-stereotyped) and others providing less such talk. Finally, there were variations in both mother and child speech as a function of child gender and gender of referent. In sum, by age 2, there is much essentialist content in mother–child conversations, even for mothers who express gender egalitarian beliefs. Mothers' linguistic input conveys subtle messages about gender from which children may construct their own essentialist beliefs.

I. INTRODUCTION

GENDER ESSENTIALISM IN CHILDREN

This *Monograph* examines essentialist concepts of gender in young children. Essentialism is the belief (often erroneous) that members of a category share an inherent, non-obvious property (essence) that confers identity and causes other category-typical properties to emerge (Medin, 1989). Essentialism is unlikely to be a wholly *accurate* belief system, yet it is pervasive in human thought (Gelman, 2003; Rehder & Hastie, 2001). It may be one of the central cognitive biases underlying stereotyping (Haslam, Rothschild, & Ernst, 2002). Gender essentialism includes a cluster of beliefs, including that observable gender differences are discovered rather than invented, biological rather than social in origins, unalterable rather than modifiable, mutually exclusive rather than overlapping, and predictive of a host of other non-obvious differences (Gelman & Taylor, 2000).

From an early age, children essentialize gender. Preschool children readily infer non-obvious characteristics of boys and girls based on their category membership (Gelman, Collman, & Maccoby, 1986). They exaggerate differences between the sexes,[1] for example, they deny or misremember gender anomalies (Liben & Signorella, 1987), at times assume that gender roles such as "mother" and "doctor" are mutually exclusive (Deák & Maratsos, 1998; but see Experiment 2), have strong affective or moral responses to gender anomalies (Levy, Taylor, & Gelman, 1995), and treat boys and girls as opposites (Martin, Eisenbud, & Rose, 1995). They also seem to assume an innate basis for gender-stereotyped traits (Taylor, 1996). These findings are consistent with other research demonstrating that preschool children hold essentialist beliefs about a range of natural categories, including animal kinds, natural substances, race, and personality characteristics (see Gelman, 2003, for a review). Indeed, children appear to be *more* strongly nativist and in some cases view gender categories as *more* fixed/immutable than adults (Taylor, 1996).

Although we suggest that *children* essentialize gender, we do not ourselves espouse essentialism as a true or accurate description of gender differences. Note that essentialism here is used in two distinct senses: as a

1

psychological construct used to characterize children's concepts, and as a metaphysical construct that makes certain assumptions about the structure of the world (namely, that male/female differences are immutable, rooted in biology, etc.).

How, when, and why children develop these beliefs about gender is a question of great significance for understanding social categorization and stereotyping. We emphasize that our claim is *not* that gender essentialism is accurate, but rather that gender essentialism is a psychological phenomenon. Children tend to essentialize gender, and the question of interest is why. Liben and Bigler (2002) review three classes of explanations that are most often provided: gender essentialism, gender environmentalism, and gender constructivism. An essentialist explanation presumes a powerful biological basis to sex and gender differences, which are then reflected in children's beliefs. A gender environmentalist explanation places great emphasis on environmental factors that model and teach gender stereotypes to children. Gender constructivism presumes that children are "active agents" (in Liben & Bigler's words) who create their own gender concepts, and do not directly reflect either biological differences or environmental messages.

We work within a gender constructivist framework. That is, we assume that gender differences are not located inherently or wholly within the individual (e.g., a girl is not born with a preference for dolls), nor are gender differences simply passively absorbed by children from environmental "input." Rather, children actively create (construct) their gender beliefs, making use of both social interactions and their own conceptual biases. Various scholars have made the important point that constructivism (or constructionism) stands in contrast to biological essentialism. For example, Bohan (1993) notes that, whereas essentialism locates gender in the individual, constructionism locates gender in social interactions. Likewise, Leaper (2000, p. 127) aptly notes: "The constructivist perspective has been compatible with the feminist argument that gender inequities are due to sexist practices rather than to inherent biological differences between women and men." However, we also emphasize that sexist practices alone do not yield gender essentialism in children; they interact with children's cognitive schemas and reasoning biases (Martin, Ruble, & Szkrybalo, 2002). Bussey and Bandura (1999) make the point that children do not passively absorb gender role conceptions from external influences, but instead, "they construct generic conceptions from the diversity of styles of conduct that are modeled, evaluatively prescribed and taught by different individuals or by even the same person for different activities in different contexts" (p. 689).

Within a constructivist framework, it is crucial to examine the messages that children receive about gender. Bohan (1993, p. 13) suggests: "Among the most forceful of factors that shape our constructions of knowledge are the modes of discourse by which we exchange our perceptions and descriptions of reality." Parents are an obvious starting point for understanding what messages children receive about gender. Most theories of gender role socialization begin with the premise that it is "the adults of each generation who pass on to each new generation of children, by means of teaching and example, the culture of gender—beliefs, myths, and rules of sex-appropriate behavior—that pervade the particular society in which the children are growing up" (Maccoby, 1998, p. 119). Surprisingly, however, when researchers have examined the relations between young children's attitudes and those of their parents, often little or no relation is found (Maccoby, 1998; Tenenbaum & Leaper, 2002). This pattern would seem to contradict social-learning theories of gender development. On the other hand, there are various reasons why such a lack of relation might be found, even if social-learning theories are valid. For example, children's perceptions of the environment may be more important than how the environment is objectively structured (Bussey & Bandura, 1999). Thus, we would not expect children's concepts to mirror the input directly, but only as filtered through their perceptions. Maccoby (1998) suggests that, in its broadest sense, socialization involves not only direct influences of parents or other agents on children, but also the child's own acquisition of stereotypes. In this view, once children know whether they are girls or boys and understand what is considered appropriate for their own gender, they can use this rich source of information to regulate their own behavior so that it fits with social standards. Children accomplish this by imitating and identifying with same-sex models, particularly those who are thought to be exemplary members of their own gender category.

A further possibility, one that has received less attention in the research literature, is that parents do play a significant role in gender-role socialization, but that they provide *implicit* rather than *explicit* messages about gender categories. Perhaps parents do not typically communicate their gender role beliefs to children in direct ways. That is, parents may only infrequently endorse gender stereotypes, whereas they may make frequent use of more implicit cues. It is therefore important to document the kinds of implicit cues parents provide (whether consciously or unconsciously) when talking to their children. Maccoby (1998) makes the case that in order to better understand the role that parents play in gender socialization, we need to turn to naturalistic situations, in which parents interact with their own infants and toddlers, and that we need to examine "what parents are talking to children about and what specific child behaviors they are responding to" (p. 122). Only then can researchers begin to investigate how such cues correspond to children's attitudes.

3

APPROACH OF THIS STUDY

The approach we take is to provide a microanalytic examination of parent-child talk about gender. By examining parent-child conversations, we are able to gain new insight on two distinct sets of questions: *First*, what are children's early beliefs? There is a rich literature on children's gender concepts at ages 4 and above, but much less is known about younger children and developmental changes in the early preschool years. Natural language conversations are a valuable tool for telling us about children's *early* concepts. Bartsch and Wellman (1995) propose that children's early conversations can be especially revealing of the conceptual distinctions they honor. Young children who may have difficulty with the demands of experimental tasks can demonstrate more capacity in conversation with family members.

Second, what information do parents provide? This is a piece of the broader question of where children's gender concepts and gender stereotypes come from. There are undoubtedly a broad range of social influences, including parents, peers, educational practices, media representations, and occupational systems (Bussey & Bandura, 1999; Calvert & Huston, 1987; Maccoby, 1998; Ruble, Balaban, & Cooper, 1981; Signorielli & Bacue, 1999). For present purposes we focus on parents, who are especially important in the preschool years.

As mentioned earlier, most prior work examining parental influences has focused on broad differences in parental beliefs, practices, and parenting styles. The view that parents play a significant role in shaping gender-typed behavior in their children is widely held among social scientists and the general public; however, converging evidence suggests that direct socialization alone does not provide an adequate account of gender development. Parents do seem to play a role during early development by offering gender-typed toys to children, by encouraging "sex-appropriate" play themes, and by engaging in more rough-and-tumble play with boys than with girls (Maccoby, 1998). However, parents show few differences towards sons and daughters on important global measures of behavior (Leaper, Anderson, & Sanders, 1998; Lytton & Romney, 1991; Maccoby, 1998). For example, they do not differ in how much they interact with their daughters and sons overall nor on amounts of positive, negative, or neutral interaction. They show similar amounts of warmth, affection, nurturance, and responsiveness, and are equally likely to be demanding, restrictive, or assertive, in their interactions with sons and daughters.

Although much of the prior work on the role of parental influences has focused on global measures of parental behavior, several of these studies include a focus on parental language. For the most part, studies that include a focus on language have examined language style, and how language is used to socialize children. For example, parents speak differently toward boys than girls about emotions, with more talk and a greater range of talk about emotions when talking to girls than when talking to boys (Dunn, Bretherton, & Munn, 1987; Kuebli, Butler, & Fivush, 1995). Mothers also provide relatively more talk about positive emotions with girls, and relatively more talk about anger with boys (Fivush, 1989). They provide more explanations of scientific content in a museum setting when talking to boys vs. girls (Crowley, Callanan, Tenenbaum, & Allen, 2001), and more talk "of the type thought to facilitate cognitive development" when talking to boys vs. girls (Weitzman, Birns, & Friend, 1985). Likewise, there are interesting sex-of-child differences in how teachers talk with young children (e.g., teachers interrupting girls more than boys; Hendrick & Stange, 1991). In an important meta-analysis, Leaper, Anderson, and Sanders (1998) examined parental talkativeness, affiliative speech, and assertive speech. Across 25 studies, Leaper et al. found that mothers talk differently than fathers (e.g., more talkative, less directive), and that mothers use more supportive speech with daughters than sons. All of these important differences could influence children's gender-related behaviors, attributes, and beliefs. For example, greater focus on causal explanations of science exhibits for boys vs. girls could contribute to gender differences in children's interest and knowledge about scientific concepts (Crowley et al., 2001).

What is much less understood is what parents say to children *about* gender per se. There is little known at this point about how parents talk about gender categories to their children, and in turn how such talk might contribute to developing gender concepts. Talk about gender is potentially important in two ways: as a means of explicit expression of gender-stereotyped beliefs, and as a means of implicit focus on gender categories. For example, consider an excerpt from an infamous children's book published in 1970 (Darrow, 1970), *I'm Glad I'm a Boy, I'm Glad I'm a Girl!*:

> Boys are doctors; Girls are nurses.
> Boys are football players; Girls are cheerleaders.
> Boys invent things; Girls use the things boys invent.
> Boys fix things; Girls need things fixed.
> Boys are presidents; Girls are first ladies.

What makes this book so offensive as to lead to banishment from library shelves and to provoke one reviewer on www.amazon.com to call it a "horrible, sexist book!"? We suspect that the book offends precisely because it so effectively recruits *multiple* devices to portray and exaggerate gender differences. The author not only expresses stereotypical activities of boys and girls in ways that argue for girls' passivity and helplessness, but also uses noun forms ("boys" and "girls" [in general]) which imply that these roles generalize broadly across an entire gender; a verb form (present, non-progressive tense) which implies that these gendered roles are timeless, enduring, and unchanging; and contrasting couplets to suggest that male and female activities are dichotomous, polarized, and opposing. Without such devices, the power of the text diminishes. For example, consider the following:

> Some boys want to be doctors or football players. I know a girl who needed something fixed. Another girl grew up to be a first lady.

This hypothetical text, although also expressing gender stereotypes, is not nearly as pointed in its portrayal of gender. Although Darrow's text is likely an extreme example, and we do not expect to find anything approaching the power of this text in the speech addressed to young children in this study (with a well-educated, middle-class U.S. sample), we also hypothesized that some of these devices would appear in the language that young children hear. We review both explicit and implicit functions of gendered language below.

LANGUAGE AS A WINDOW ONTO GENDER CONCEPTS

Considering both explicit and implicit messages, there are several possible ways that talk about gender may be used to convey gender concepts. We review five possible sources of information, each of which has been identified in past research that is reviewed below: (1) endorsing or rejecting gender stereotypes; (2) providing gender labels; (3) contrasting males vs. females; (4) expressing gender equality; and (5) expressing generic categories of gender.

Endorsing (or Rejecting) Gender Stereotypes

The most straightforward and direct way of conveying gender-typed information is to endorse gender stereotypes. A speaker can use language to express the belief that an individual of a given sex, or members of that gender category in general, are appropriate for a given activity. Likewise, a speaker can use language to express the belief that an individual of a given sex, or members of that gender category in general, are *not* appropriate for a given activity. A statement such as a boy saying, "I'm going to be a firefighter when I grow up," or the infamous talking Barbie who said, "Math is hard" are examples of stated gender stereotypes. Statements such as these can either reinforce or contradict parallel non-linguistic information in the environment (e.g., scarcity of women firefighters; girls performing just as well as boys in elementary-school math). Language may also make more explicit and salient information that otherwise would not be represented in terms of gender.

Numerous studies have found that parents encourage gender-typed toy play, discourage cross-gender toy play (e.g., refraining from offering a doll to a boy), and reward gender-typed play (Eisenberg, Wolchik, Hernandez, & Pasternack, 1985; Fagot, 1978; Fagot, Hagan, Leinbach, & Kronsberg, 1985; see Lytton & Romney, 1991, for a review and meta-analysis). These studies often include both behaviors and language; for example, a parent's response might be coded as "positive," whether it is a smile, hug, or verbal praise. However, the gender-typing messages conveyed by language are not usually examined separately. Thus, to our knowledge it is not clear how often and in what contexts children receive these explicit gender-typing messages in parental language.

Providing Gender Labels

Much work in the language development literature suggests that providing a label highlights categories for children (e.g., Baldwin, Markman, & Melartin, 1993; Gelman & Heyman, 1999; Waxman, 1999; Waxman & Markow, 1995; Welder & Graham, 2001; Xu, 1999, 2002; see Gelman, 2003, for review). Hearing a common label for objects highlights their categorical relatedness, and encourages children to treat instances as being alike in non-obvious ways. This is true for a wide range of labels, including words for animals (Gelman & Markman, 1986), trait labels (Heyman & Gelman, 2000), and gender labels (Bauer & Coyne, 1997; Gelman, Collman, & Maccoby, 1986). Therefore, use of gender labels is potentially an important means of emphasizing gender categories.

Clear effects of language are found when researchers have examined how children interpret different forms of reference to gender. Children interpret gendered labels as implying that an activity is exclusive to one sex (e.g., "policeman" is interpreted as exclusively male by school-aged children; Liben, Bigler, & Krogh, 2002), and they interpret generic use of the pronoun "he" as referring exclusively to males (Hyde, 1984). Interestingly, mothers display a male bias in labeling of gender-neutral animal characters in a picture book (DeLoache, Cassidy, & Carpenter, 1987). This finding suggests that mothers may use language in a way that highlights males more than females, contributing to a tendency for language to ignore women (Henley, 1989).

Contrasting Males vs. Females

Young children have a tendency to treat categories as contrasting or mutually exclusive (Markman, 1989; Clark, 1987; but see Deák & Maratsos, 1998), and this is particularly so for gender categories (e.g., Martin, 1989;

Martin, Eisenbud, & Rose, 1995). In other words, children often seem to assume that if something is appropriate for girls, then it is not appropriate for boys, and vice versa. One way to convey this idea is by means of direct contrasts: X is for girls, not boys. Even 2-year-olds are sensitive to linguistic means of expressing such contrasts. For example, Waxman and Klibanoff (2000) find that providing a contrasting negative example helps children learn a new word (see also Au & Laframboise, 1990; Gottfried & Tonks, 1996). Interestingly, children provide contrasts for a variety of important concepts as early as 2 or 3 years of age (e.g., talk about mental states by contrasting belief vs. reality, Shatz, Wellman, & Silber, 1983; Bartsch & Wellman, 1995; reasoning about food, Nguyen & Murphy, 2003). Even adults sometimes treat graded categories as dichotomous (e.g., treating certain food substances as either wholly good or wholly bad; Rozin, Ashmore, & Markwith, 1996). Comparing instances may also help children align gender categories to enable a sharper contrast (see Gentner & Namy, 2000; Markman & Gentner, 2000, for fuller discussion of the importance of structural alignment more generally). Conversely, providing training with *multiple* classifications (e.g., sorting pictures of people by gender, and by occupation), which differ in structure from binary contrasts, leads to greater flexibility and less gender stereotyping (Bigler & Liben, 1992). Little is known, however, regarding when parents and children produce talk that contrasts boys with girls or men with women.

Expressing Gender Equality

One can use language to convey that an activity is appropriate to both genders. This is the reverse of highlighting gender differences. Such expressions are a direct means of countering gender stereotypes. Past research has found that parents differ in the degree of positive or negative reactions they provide for gender-typed behavior (Leaper, 2002). These studies suggest that some parents tolerate cross-gender-typed behavior, and therefore may be endorsing gender equality. However, little is known about the frequency of such talk among parents or children.

Expressing Generic Categories

In recent work on children's essentialist beliefs about animals, we have found that parents provide little *explicit* essentialist talk about categories (i.e., parents rarely if ever talk about non-obvious internal similarities, or innate capacities), yet they provide much *implicit* essentialist talk in the form of generic noun phrases (Gelman et al., 1998). Generic noun phrases express category-wide generalizations; they refer to a category as an abstract whole (Carlson & Pelletier, 1995). For example, compare the generic sentence *"Girls* play with dolls" with the non-generic sentence *"Those girls* are playing with dolls." In the first sentence, and in contrast to the second, "girls" refers to the abstract set of girls in general. Furthermore, generics typically refer to qualities that are relatively stable (non-accidental), enduring (not transient), and timeless (not contextually bound) (Lyons, 1977). Use of a generic thus implies that a category is a coherent, stable entity. In English, generic noun phrases are expressed with bare plurals (e.g., "*Bats* live in caves"), definite singulars (e.g., "*The elephant* is found in Africa and Asia"), or indefinite articles (e.g., "*A male goose* is called a gander"), and are accompanied by present-tense verbs.

Unlike utterances containing universal quantifiers such as *all, every,* or *each,* generic statements allow for exceptions. Whereas even a single counterexample would negate the generalization "All boys play with trucks", the generic statement "Boys play with trucks" can persist in the face of counterexamples (Hollander, Gelman, & Star, 2002). Thus, we hypothesize that the dual nature of generics (as attributed to most members of a category but robust against counter-evidence) means that properties expressed with generics will be particularly persistent in children's developing knowledge systems. Generics may highlight similarities among members of a gender category for young children and promote essentialist beliefs.

Children produce generics in spontaneous interactions with their parents as young as 2-1/2 years of age (Gelman, 2003; Pappas & Gelman, 1998). By 2 to 3 years of age, children also interpret generics differently from nongenerics (e.g., "Do birds fly?" vs. "Do the birds fly?"). Importantly, prior work has found that when 4-year-old children hear generics, they interpret them as broader in scope than "some" but narrower in scope than "all" (Hollander, Gelman, & Star, 2002). For example, if asked about bears having white fur, they are most likely to say that *some* bears have white fur, least likely to say that *all* bears have white fur, and moderately likely to say that *bears* have white fur. Furthermore, when 4-year-olds hear new facts stated in generic form, they generalize the facts to new instances more broadly than when it is said to be true of "some" members, and less broadly than when it is said to be true of "all" members. Thus, generics appear to be interpreted as referring to general categories by preschool age.

Of particular relevance to the present context, studies that provide generic (category-wide) prompts to children about gender (e.g., "I think *boys* like the things in this box better than *girls* do"; "The game is for *girls,* like jacks"), lead children to modify their play behavior to conform to the gender stereotype (Bradbard & Endsley, 1983), to recall more information about toys labeled for the child's own gender (Bradbard, Martin, Endsley, & Halverson, 1986), and to find the activity more attractive when labeled for the child's own sex (Montemayor, 1974). However, such studies were not focused on the linguistic distinction between generics and non-generics, and so did not provide a direct contrast between the two forms of speech.

At this point little is known about the generics that children produce or hear concerning gender (though see Gelman & Taylor, 2000, for a preliminary investigation of this issue). Some evidence suggests that among preschool-aged children, one or two instances can be sufficient to prompt a gender-related generic (Martin, Ruble, & Szkrybalo, 2002, p. 925). For example, Martin et al. describe an anecdote originally reported by Bjorklund (2000, p. 362), in which a child concluded "Men eat pizza and women don't" after a trip to a restaurant in which his father and another male ordered pizza and his mother ordered lasagna. At the same time, prior research suggests that there may be important developmental shifts in the relative importance of gender (category) information vs. individuating information, in how children reason about people. For example, Biernat (1991) gave children ranging from kindergarten age through 10th grade and college students descriptions of boys or girls with either stereotypical attributes (e.g., a girl who babysits) or counter-stereotypical attributes (e.g., a girl who plays baseball), and asked them to judge which other characteristics each child would have. At all ages participants used gender labels (whether the target child was a "boy" or a "girl"), but as children got older, they were increasingly likely to use individuating information (e.g., whether the child babysits or plays baseball). An examination of gender-referring generics in children's speech, and in the speech that children hear, is a needed next step in determining children's use of generic categories in the speech they hear and produce.

STUDY OVERVIEW

To examine gender talk in mother–child conversations, we videotaped mothers and their young children (2, 4, or 6 years of age) discussing a picture book that depicted stereotypical and counter-stereotypical gendered activities (e.g., a boy playing football; a boy sewing). These interactions were transcribed, coded, and analyzed in fine-grained detail. Mothers and children also completed tasks that measured gender stereotyping and/ or gender constancy.

These ages were selected for two reasons. First, during the preschool years, parental input is an especially important source of information to children (Sabbagh & Callanan, 1998). This is also true with gender-related talk. In their meta-analysis of parents' child-directed language, Leaper, Anderson, and Sanders (1998) find that variations in how parents talk to girls vs. boys was greatest for young children (infants and toddlers), when the highest rate of language learning is taking place. Second and equally important, the ages from 2 to 6 years represent an important period for gender development. Knowledge of gender categories and stereotypes increases rapidly in the second year and continues to undergo significant changes during the preschool and kindergarten years. Traditionally, gender constancy, or at least knowledge of one's own gender, was thought to be a prerequisite for acquiring gender stereotypes, however, more recently, researchers have argued that only rudimentary, implicit gender concepts (e.g., discrimination between males and females) may be needed to get the process started (Serbin, Poulin-Dubois, Colburne, Sen, & Eichstedt, 2001). Most children correctly apply gender labels to themselves and others by the time they are 30 to 36 months—some by 24 months (Fagot & Leinbach, 1995)—and they are soon proficient at gender categorization (Johnston, Madole, Bittinger, & Smith, 2000; Katz, 1996; Leinbach & Fagot, 1986; Levy, 1999; Stipek, Gralinski, & Kopp, 1990; Poulin-Dubois, Serbin, & Derbyshire, 1998).

Toddlers also have at least an implicit knowledge of gender stereotyping, even before they acquire gender constancy, and understand that the characteristics associated with gender (e.g., activities, toys, occupations, hairstyles, and clothing) do not determine whether a person is female or male. Eighteen-month-old girls showed preferential looking for a face that matched the gender-stereotyping of a previously presented toy (Serbin et al., 2001). In addition to stereotyping toys, toddlers also have begun to form metaphorical gender associations, such as linking bears, fir trees, and the color blue with males (Eichstedt, Serbin, Poulin-Dubois, & Sen, 2000). By the preschool years, children have extensive knowledge about the characteristics associated with gender categories (Edelbrock & Sugawara, 1978; Kuhn, Nash, & Brucken, 1978; Ruble & Martin, 1998), and they make stereotypical inferences readily on the basis of sex (Bauer & Coyne, 1997; Gelman, Collman, & Maccoby, 1986).

One issue we can address in this study is what sorts of changes with age we find in children's and parents' talk about gender. For example, is there a steadily increasing amount of attention to gender, or are there sudden "jumps" over time? Does attention to gender show a monotonic increase, or does it peak and then level off or drop? Do changes in children's focus on gender correspond to change in maternal input? How do changes in gender constancy, or gender stereotyping on traditional measures, correspond to the talk between mothers and children? By studying three distinct age groups over this rapidly changing period, we can examine these issues.

The picture-book reading task was chosen as one that is a relatively unstructured, naturalistic, and frequent form of interaction, and therefore one that we hoped would enable a fairly representative sample of the conversations that mothers and children have about gender. Book-reading has been used in prior studies of parent-child conversations (Callanan, 1985, 1990; DeLoache & DeMendoza, 1987; Gelman, Coley, Rosengren, et al., 1998; Pappas & Gelman, 1998; Murphy, 1978; Snow & Goldfield, 1983; Wheeler, 1983; Ninio, 1980; van Kleeck, Stahl, & Bauer, 2003), revealing interesting developmental and individual variation, and so enables comparison to past work.

As noted above, we varied the consistency of the page, that is, whether the person-activity pairing is gender-stereotype-*consistent* (e.g., boy playing football) or gender-stereotype-*inconsistent* (e.g., boy sewing). This was done in order to present scenarios that, as a group, equally affirm and negate gender stereotypes, so as not to be biased in either direction. By doing so, we are able to discover what speakers bring to the interaction. For example, if speakers tend to make more gender-stereotyping than anti-stereotyping comments, this would be *despite* information in the book, which is no more biased toward stereotyping than against it. Also, researchers have at times speculated about how gender-neutral materials might modify children's stereotyping (e.g., Bem, 1983; see Bigler, 1999, for review). By varying the materials, we can assess whether and how parent and child talk reflects the exemplars that are available.

A recurrent issue throughout the analyses concerns the importance of child sex, and the importance of sex-of-referent (i.e., whether the speaker is talking about a male or a female). Maccoby (1998) argues that sex-linked behavior is a "pervasive function of the social context in which it occurs" (p. 9) and that the optimal level of analysis is the dyad rather than the individual. A variety of studies have found that parents speak differently to sons than to daughters (e.g., Gleason, 1987; see Leaper et al., 1998, for review). It will be interesting to examine whether the messages mothers provide about gender differ for sons vs. daughters. We included equal numbers of boys and girls at each age, to enable a direct comparison of child sex in all analyses. Furthermore, we analyzed data by sex-of-referent. There is converging evidence that, at least in this culture at this historical point, stereotypes regarding males tend to be more rigid and restrictive than stereotypes regarding females (e.g., Hort, Fagot, & Leinbach, 1990), that males change gender typing and gender roles less often and less easily than females (Katz, 1986), and that, from early on, males play a more active role in bringing about and maintaining the separation of the sexes in social interactions (Maccoby, 1998). Females can take on male roles, activities, or behaviors with less censure than males taking on female roles, and parents show more tolerance for stereotypically masculine behavior in girls and more concern about appropriate gender typing in boys (Katz, 1986). It will therefore be important to determine whether and how these differences are conveyed in natural language.

12

RESEARCH QUESTIONS

The monograph addresses three primary questions, all concerned in one way or another with the goals laid out earlier: to examine children's early gender beliefs and mothers' gender-relevant talk. These questions are as follows:

How and in what contexts do children and mothers express gender essentialism or gender equality?

This is the primary question addressed in this research. "How" refers to means of expression. We examine six primary means by which mothers and children could reveal attention to gender and/or gender stereotypes: (a) gender-stereotypical content, (b) reference to gendered *categories* (by means of generic noun phrases) as opposed to gendered *individuals*, (c) gender labeling, (d) gender contrasts, (e) naming accuracy and naming errors, and (f) gender equality. "In what contexts" is an issue concerning characteristics of the individual (whether the speaker is the mother or the child; age and sex of the child), characteristics of the picture book context (whether a page depicts stereotypical vs. counter-stereotypical activities), and characteristics of the referent (male vs. female). We also explore the relative frequency of gender references and age references, to determine the salience of gender as compared to another highly important social category.

How does talk about categories differ from talk about individuals (generics vs. non-generics)?

Given the frequency and centrality of generics in mother–child speech, we wished to know how distinctive generics are, in the information they convey. We therefore examine differences between generics and non-generics regarding: (a) content, (b) form, and (c) modality.

What are the discourse patterns in mother–child conversations?

The analyses described above focus on children and mothers separately, analyzing the content and form of their speech considered independently of one another. In contrast, this third question concerns the nature of the mother–child interactions. Three issues are of particular interest: First, how do mothers respond to child stereotyping? Second, who leads the way in introducing generics—children or mothers? Third, how highly do mothers and children correlate with one another in the nature of the talk they provide? We will also examine how mother–child conversations compare to their scores on tasks measuring gender-typing and gender constancy, to explore whether individual differences in mother or child talk significantly predict individual differences on these more standard measures.

NOTE

1. Appropriate use of the terms "sex" and "gender" is a topic of current debate (e.g., Gentile, 1993). In this monograph, we use the term "sex" to refer to a person as male or female (e.g., child sex, sex of referent) and "gender" to refer to properties commonly assumed to have a sociocultural basis (see Unger, 1979).

II. METHODS AND PRELIMINARY RESULTS

PARTICIPANTS

Participants were 72 mother–child dyads, 24 at each of three child ages: 2 years (range 2.4–3.0; mean age 2.7), 4 years (range 4.0–5.0; mean age 4.7), and 6 years (range 6.1–7.0; mean age 6.7). Half the children at each age were girls, half were boys. The majority of the participants were white (94% of mothers, 92% of children); the remaining were ethnic or racial minorities (Asian, African-American, or other). Approximately one-third of the mothers indicated that they did not work outside the home ($N = 7$ at age 2 years, 10 at age 4 years, and 9 at age 6 years). Twenty university undergraduates provided ratings to help us pre-select the activities that would be depicted in the picture book.

Table 1 presents basic descriptive data regarding age and educational level of the parents, as well as number of siblings in the family. We conducted a 3 (age group: 2, 4, 6 years) × 2 (child sex: boy, girl) MANOVA, with mother's age, mother's education, father's age, father's education, and number of siblings as dependent variables. Education was based on a score ranging from 1 to 6, where 1 = some high school, 2 = high school diploma, 3 = technical or trade training, 4 = some college, 5 = college degree, and 6 = post-college education. The analysis indicated a main effect for age group, $F(10, 122) = 2.11$, $p < .05$, but no main effect for child sex, and no age group × child sex interaction. The effect of age group was located in three of the five dependent variables: mother's age ($F(2, 65) = 5.99$, $p < .005$), father's age ($F(2, 65) = 8.57$, $p < .001$), and number of siblings ($F(2, 65) = 3.30$, $p < .05$). Mothers of 2-year-olds were younger than mothers of 4- or 6-year-olds, both $ps < .05$ by Bonferroni tests. (Unless otherwise stated, Bonferroni tests are used in all follow-up t-tests.) Similarly, fathers of 2-year-olds were younger than fathers of 4- or 6-year-olds, both $ps < .005$. Finally, 2-year-olds had fewer siblings than 6-year-olds, $p < .05$. These differences are expected, given the cohort differences between families with 2-year-olds and families with older children. Most importantly, child sex was not correlated with any demographic differences, and child age did not correspond to differences in parent education. We can therefore be

TABLE 1

FAMILY DEMOGRAPHICS AS A FUNCTION OF CHILD AGE AND CHILD SEX

Child Age/Sex	Mother's Age	Father's Age	Mother's Education[a]	Father's Education[a]	Number of Siblings
2 years-boy	34.73	34.09	5.45	5.36	1.00
	(4.24)	(4.68)	(0.69)	(0.81)	(0.89)
2 years-girl	36.33	37.17	5.67	5.42	1.00
	(5.23)	(6.87)	(0.65)	(1.00)	(0.95)
4 years-boy	40.00	41.83	5.17	5.00	1.17
	(4.80)	(5.11)	(1.19)	(1.21)	(0.83)
4 years-girl	39.17	41.00	5.42	5.42	1.42
	(4.28)	(4.95)	(0.51)	(0.90)	(0.51)
6 years-boy	39.33	41.08	5.33	5.25	1.75
	(3.31)	(4.87)	(0.89)	(0.87)	(1.14)
6 years-girl	38.50	40.33	5.25	5.42	1.58
	(3.34)	(4.31)	(0.87)	(1.00)	(0.90)

Note.—SDs are in parentheses.

[a]On a scale from 1 to 6, where 1 = some high school, 2 = high school diploma, 3 = technical or trade training, 4 = some college, 5 = college degree, and 6 = post-college education.

reassured that any results we obtain for child age or child sex in the main study cannot be attributed to these factors.

MATERIALS

The primary task was based on one that researchers have used successfully in the past to investigate concepts outside of the domain of gender: parent–child picture-book reading. We created four books with the following specifications. Each book had 16 pages: eight pages depicting males, eight pages depicting females. Each page portrayed a behavior, occupation, or activity that is typically associated with one gender or the other. The drawings were brightly colored and moderately realistic. Half the pages were gender-consistent (e.g., boys playing football), and half were gender-inconsistent (e.g., boys playing with dolls). Each page had text printed that asked "Who can X?," where X was the activity of the page (e.g., "Who can chop wood?" "Who can play with dolls?").

We created four versions of the book, so that the "male" pages in one book were the "female" pages in the other book (and vice versa), and so that the order of the pages varied. For example, one book depicted a man firefighter and a boy playing with dolls, whereas the other book depicted a woman firefighter and a girl playing with dolls. The male and female versions of each activity page were identical (in layout, color, background,

16

TABLE 2

COMPLETE SET OF ACTIVITIES DEPICTED IN THE PICTURE BOOKS

FEMININE—child	FEMININE—adult
Play with dolls (4.35)	Knit (4.40)
Pick flowers (4.20)	Feed a baby (3.75)
Play hopscotch (4.10)	Do aerobics (3.95)
Sew (4.40)	Be a seamstress (4.38)
Help bake cookies (3.90)	Be a cheerleader (3.90)
Dust (4.00)	Be a ballet dancer (3.85)
MASCULINE—child	MASCULINE—adult
Play football (1.60)	Chop wood (1.65)
Play with trucks (1.75)	Paint the house (1.95)
Catch frogs (2.10)	Drive a truck (2.00)
Fix a bike (1.70)	Be a race car driver (1.65)
Deliver a newspaper (2.10)	Be a sailor (1.85)
Take out the trash (2.15)	Be a firefighter (1.85)

Note.—Adult ratings from the pretest are provided in parentheses (1 = only boys/men; 5 = only girls/ women).

and details) except for the gender of the character (e.g., man vs. woman firefighter), as indicated by hair length, facial hair, and/or clothing. Overall, participants had equal opportunity to talk about gender-consistent and gender-inconsistent behaviors. See Table 2 for complete set of activities depicted in the picture books, and Figures 1–4 for two sample pictures, each in both male and female formats.[2]

Who can chop wood?

FIGURE 1

17

Who can chop wood?

FIGURE 2

Pretesting of Items

In order to select a set of activities that would be strongly gender-stereotyped, we pretested a set of 70 activities on 20 undergraduate students. The undergraduates rated each activity on a 5-point scale (1 = only boys/men; 3 = both boys/men and girls/women; 5 = only girls/women). Based on the ratings, we selected 12 stereotypically male and 12 stereotypically female activities for use in the picture book. The stereotypically male

Who can be a cheerleader?

FIGURE 3

Who can be a cheerleader?

FIGURE 4

activities selected for the picture book ranged from 1.60 to 2.15 on the scale, with a mean of 1.86; the stereotypically female activities selected for the picture book ranged from 3.75 to 4.40, with a mean of 4.10. All 20 adults gave higher ratings for the female activities than for the male activities, $p < .001$ by sign test.

Gender-typing and Gender Constancy Measures

After completing the book-reading task, mothers and children completed a set of tasks designed to assess gender constancy (in children) and gender-typing (in both children and mothers). These tasks were included in order to examine whether talk during the book-reading task corresponds to gender beliefs as assessed in a more controlled context. We predicted that gendered conversations would correlate with gender beliefs: mothers who provide more consistent gender-stereotyped messages in their talk were predicted to be more stereotyped on their attitudes and preferences; children who provide more consistent gender-stereotyped messages in their talk were predicted to be more stereotyped and to have higher gender constancy scores (see Martin et al., 2002, for discussion of the role of gender constancy in children's gender concepts). However, we could also find that how people *talk* about gender bears little relation to their attitudes and beliefs. For example, mothers might restrict the amount of explicit gender-typing messages they provide if they think such messages are socially inappropriate. Conversely, it may be that *implicit* expressions of gender are so automatic, unconscious, and basic, that they appear widely, regardless of stereotyping beliefs. An examination of cross-task correlations (reading compared to gender-typing) is needed to examine how natural language corresponds to those other measures.

Children received two sorts of measures: a test of gender-stereotype flexibility and a test of gender constancy. Mothers received measures of gender attitudes (a questionnaire asking "who should" have certain occupations, activities, and traits: men, women, or both) and of personal relevance (a questionnaire asking which occupations they would most like; and which activities and traits are most descriptive of themselves). These measures were based on the OAT (Liben & Bigler, 2002). They also received a few questions regarding their own and their spouse's (or partner's) age, educational level, and occupation, as well as the number of other children in the family and their age and sex.

Gender Labeling Task (2-Year-Olds Only)

Two-year-olds received a simple gender labeling task that asked them to match gendered names and labels to gendered pictures (from Kuhn, Nash, & Brucken, 1978). There were 16 items, 4 each for a boy, a girl, a man, and a woman. See Appendix A for the full set of questions.

Child Gender-stereotype Flexibility Task (4- and 6-Year-olds Only)[3]

The items on the test of gender-stereotype flexibility were deliberately chosen so as not to overlap with any of the items presented in the picture book. The reason for this is that we wanted a measure that was uncontaminated by the immediately prior book-reading session (either the maternal input or the pictures themselves). We selected items for the flexibility task that received clearly male or clearly female ratings on either our adult pre-test measure (see "Pretesting of items" above) or the COAT (Liben & Bigler, 2002). These items are presented in Appendix B.

This task included 16 gender-stereotyped items (four each for boy, girl, man, and woman) and four gender-neutral items. The gender-neutral items were included only for the sake of including variation in the stimulus set, and were not analyzed further. Four- and 6-year-olds had three options for each item: "boys," "girls," and "boys and girls" (for child activities); or "men," "women," and "men and women" (for adult activities). To make the task more engaging, children were presented with a gumball machine filled with 20 marbles. For each question, children retrieved a marble from the gumball machine, listened to the question (e.g., "Who should mow the lawn?"), and then placed the marble in one of the three boxes to indicate their response. This task was intended as a measure of gender flexibility, as assessed by the frequency with which a child chose *both* sexes for any given activity. However, one limitation of the task is that it is also possible that children might at times select the "both" response because they are unfamiliar with the cultural stereotype.

Child Gender Constancy Measure (Self)

All age groups received a gender constancy measure that was slightly modified from Kuhn et al.'s (1978) task. All questions concerned the child's own gender constancy. They were asked the following questions: (1) "When you were a little baby, were you a little boy or a little girl?"; (2) "Are you a boy or a girl?"; (3) "When you're 10, will you be a boy or a girl?"; (4) "When you grow up, will you be a man or a woman?"; (5) "If you have children when you grow up, will you be a daddy or a mommy?"; (6) "If you wanted to, could you be a daddy/mommy [other sex than child] when you grow up?"

Child Gender Constancy Measure (Non-self; 4- and 6-Year-olds Only)

Four- and 6-year-olds also received a constancy measure that was modified from Bem's (1989) task. Children saw a picture of a baby in a diaper, were told its gender (boy or girl), and then were asked a series of questions regarding whether the child would change gender if he/she wore clothes appropriate to the other sex, and if he/she changed back into his/her regular clothes. We coded responses to the two key questions: "What does X look like, a boy or a girl?" and "What is X really, a boy or a girl?" Each question was asked after the initial transformation and again after the baby was changed back into regular clothes, for each of two different items (a boy and a girl item), yielding a total of eight questions (2 questions × 2 transformations × 2 items). The full protocol is provided in Appendix C.

Maternal Gender-typing Measures

Mothers received the short version of the OAT (Liben & Bigler, 2002), with the addition of those items that children received on the gender- flexibility task which were not already on the OAT (short version). This change was made to permit some overlap between the child and parent measures. The original OAT items constituted a large majority of the items on the modified measure (85%). Although we added in slightly more male than female items, the overall numbers of items were very close (70 female items,

21

72 male items). In any case, the results were analyzed separately for male vs. female items, so that the slight imbalance would not bias the results. An examination of our data also revealed extremely high correlations between the original OAT and the modified version (.997 for OAT-AM/male items, .993 for OAT-AM/female items, .973 for OAT-PM/male items, and .979 for OAT-PM/female items). Therefore, we will present the data from the full set of questions. See Appendix D.

PROCEDURE

Mother–child dyads were tested in our on-campus lab. Mother and child were seated on a comfortable couch, and mothers were instructed to look through and talk about the picture book with their child, as they would normally do at home. Mothers were informed ahead of time that they would be videotaped and that we were interested in mother–child interactions; however, they were not specifically told that we were interested in language or gender until after the entire session was completed. After each video-taping session, mother and child were administered the gender-typing and gender constancy measures separately.

TRANSCRIPTIONS AND CODING

Each session was transcribed by one coder and checked twice by two additional coders. Intelligible utterances were transcribed verbatim; unintelligible utterances were also noted. The unit of analysis for transcribing and coding was the utterance. Utterances were defined as continuous units of conversation so identified according to content and intonational contour. *Continuous* was defined as being free of full stops or interruptions from the other speaker. As such, utterances consisted of sentences, phrases, or even words if they were pronounced with final pitch (rising or falling intonation). For cases in which intonation and pausing conflicted with one another, intonational cues were used. For run-on sentences, often characterized by a change of subject, the speech was divided into two or more utterances (Snow, 1972). Finally, stylistic features such as "filler" words (*OK, and, yeah*) and tag questions were combined with adjacent speech segments, unless intonation indicated that they were clearly distinct. This guideline was adopted to avoid extreme estimates of total number of utterances for participants who use these features often.

The transcripts were then coded according to the system described in this section (see Table 3). For all but one aspect of coding, two coders naive

TABLE 3

HIERARCHICAL ORGANIZATION OF CODING CATEGORIES USED TO ANALYZE THE
CONVERSATIONS

I. Focus of utterance

   A. On-task with person reference

      1. Scope

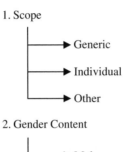

      2. Gender Content

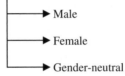

      3. Gender Form

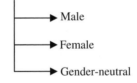

      4. Age Form

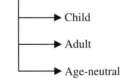

      5. Gender Ostensive Labeling

      6. Gender Contrast

      7. Gender Equality

TABLE 3

(CONTINUED)

8. Target Activity (explicit)

a. Modality

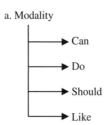

- Can
- Do
- Should
- Like

b. Valence

- Positive
- Negative
- Question/Neutral

c. Stereotyping (derived from gender content, valence, and page set-up)

- Neutral
- Negate
- Affirm

    (1) Maternal response to child's affirmations

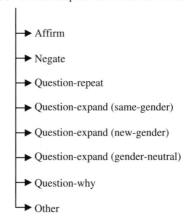

- Affirm
- Negate
- Question-repeat
- Question-expand (same-gender)
- Question-expand (new-gender)
- Question-expand (gender-neutral)
- Question-why
- Other

TABLE 3

(CONTINUED)

B. On-task without person reference

   1. Target Activity (implicit)

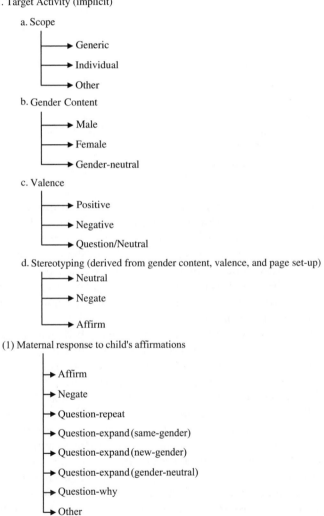

      a. Scope

            Generic

            Individual

            Other

      b. Gender Content

            Male

            Female

            Gender-neutral

      c. Valence

            Positive

            Negative

            Question/Neutral

      d. Stereotyping (derived from gender content, valence, and page set-up)

            Neutral

            Negate

            Affirm

   (1) Maternal response to child's affirmations

            Affirm

            Negate

            Question-repeat

            Question-expand (same-gender)

            Question-expand (new-gender)

            Question-expand (gender-neutral)

            Question-why

            Other

C. Off-task or unintelligible

D. Reading

TABLE 4

INTERRATER RELIABILITY ON THE CODING CATEGORIES EXPRESSED AS PERCENT AGREEMENT
AND COHEN'S KAPPAS

Coding category	% Agreement	Cohen's Kappa
Focus of utterance	94	.91
Scope	98	.91
Gender content	94	.90
Gender form	94	.92
Age form	96	.91
Gender-ostensive labeling	98	.93
Gender contrast	98	.72
Gender equality	98	.85
Target activity	89	.76
Target activity: modality	96	.89
Target activity: valence	97	.94
Maternal responses to child stereotyping:	93	.88

Note.—Descriptions of the coding categories can be found in Table 5.

to the hypotheses under investigation coded each transcript, and discrepancies were resolved by discussion between the coders. The exception was coding of maternal responses to child stereotyping, for which 25% of the transcripts were coded by two coders, and the remaining transcripts were coded by a single coder. Cohen's kappas were calculated for each coding category, on a randomly selected 25% of dyads of each age and child gender ($N = 18$) and are reported (along with percent agreement) in Table 4. See Table 5 for examples of the coding.

Each utterance was initially coded for *focus*, thus enabling us to identify on-task utterances vs. all other utterances. An utterance was considered on-task if it referred to anything in the picture book, or anything broadly related to the people or target activity depicted in the book. On-task utterances included both those referring to a person (e.g., "Are boys allowed to be ballet dancers?")[4] and those not referring to a person (e.g., "No" in response to the ballet-dancer question above). The utterances that were not coded as on-task included: off-task utterances (for example, talking about the microphone, or procedural details such as turning the pages), unintelligible utterances, or instances where the mother or child read the text of the book verbatim. Only on-task utterances were coded further and analyzed.

Each noun phrase referring to a person or persons was coded for *scope*, *gender content*, *gender form*, and *age form*. Scope refers to the generality of the referent, either an individual or set of individuals, a generic category (e.g., men in general; this included generic noun phrases only), or other (e.g., "who"; "anybody"). Of particular interest is the distinction between generic and specific scope. Gender content involves the sex of the person referred

TABLE 5

EXAMPLES OF CODING CATEGORIES USED TO CODE THE MOTHER–CHILD CONVERSATIONS

Focus of utterance (whether utterance is on- or off-task, and whether utterance explicitly refers to a person)
On-task with person reference: "Yeah, she can take out the trash."; "Uh, I can"; " That's a man chopping wood isn't he?"
On-task without person reference: "Yeah"; "That's a hammer!"; "What is that [pointing to the ocean]?"
Off-task or unintelligible: "Look at my owie"; "Oops wait, we skipped a page."
Reading: "Who can play hopscotch?"

Scope (generality of the referent)
Generic: "Dads can [paint a house]"; "A sailor is someone who's on a boat."
Individual(s): "Who is that?"; "Opa was a sailor."; "Does [female name] catch frogs?"; "Me!" [in response to, "Who can chop wood?"]; "Alright, did you think at [female name] 's ballet recital, did you see some boys dancing?"
Other: "Do you know anybody that drives a truck?"; "So, anybody could? [do aerobics]"

Gender content (gender of the referent)
Male: "Remember you used to hold her and give her her bottle" [mother talking to son; target activity was "feed a baby"]
Female: "Do you remember seeing Grandma, knit?"

Gender-neutral: "Where was the cheerleader?"; "So probably children shouldn't be holding an axe?"

Gender form (gender expressed in the wording)
Male: "Oh, what is he doing?"
Female: "Can that girl fix a bike?"
Gender-neutral: "Ohh now this one, what is this person doing?"

Age form (age expressed in the wording)
Child: "boy"; "kid"
Adult: "grown-up"; "Grandma"
Age-neutral: "they"; "ballet dancer"

Gender-ostensive labeling (explicitly commenting on gender of person in book)
"That's a girl"; "There's a boy"; "Is that a he or a she?"

Gender contrast (contrasting male and female with one another)
"That's for girls, not boys"; "Is that a girl job or a boy job?"

Gender equality (mentioning that both males and females can engage in activity)
"Anyone can do it"; "Both boys and girls can do it."

Target activity (utterances referring to gender-stereotyped activity depicted in book)
"Would an old woman be able to pick up the ax?" [explicit reference to chopping wood]; "Nope" [in response to "Would an old woman be able to pick up the ax?"; implicit reference to chopping wood]

Target activity: modality (expressing the possibility of the activity depicted in the book)
Can/ability: "Who would be able to fix a bike?"
Do/are: "Do you play with dolls?"
Should/safety: "Boys should not play with dolls"; "It's only a safe thing for adults to do that"
Prefer/like to: "I like baking cookies."

TABLE 5

(CONTINUED)

Target activity: valence (*positive, negative, or neutral attitude expressed regarding the activity depicted in the book*)
Positive: "I can do that."
Negative: "Grandma doesn't sew."
Question/Neutral: "You think dolls are for girls?"

Maternal responses to child stereotyping (*how mother responds to gender-stereotyped statements made by the child*)
Affirm: "Mm-hm"; "Yes"; "You don't want to bake cookies" [in response to: "I don't want to"]
Negate: "I think Jill [pseudonym] would have fun" [in response to child saying that Jill cannot be a race-car driver]; "You have trucks" [in response to: "I don't have any trucks"]
Question-repeat: "Daddy can be a sailor?"
Question-expand[a]: "Would you like to catch a frog?"
Question-why: "How come?"; "Well why couldn't I chop wood if I'm a girl?"
Other: "Does that look like him?"; [or, no direct response from mother]

Note.—All examples were actual quotations taken directly from the transcripts.
[a]Question-expand was subdivided into "same gender," "new gender," or "gender-neutral" with respect to the child's utterance.

to (female, male, or non-gendered). The gender form of an utterance refers to what the wording explicitly stated about the sex of the referent. For example, if the mother says, "I can drive a truck," the content would be female, but the form would be unspecified with regard to gender. The age form of an utterance refers to what the wording explicitly stated about the age group of the referent (as child or adult). For example, "That's a man" indicates that the referent is an adult. There is a potential ambiguity in same cases, especially with the word "girl," which is sometimes used to mark both age and gender (i.e., a female child) and other times is used to mark gender only (i.e., a female of any age). To be conservative, we coded all uses of "girl" and "boy" as marking both age and gender.

Furthermore, each noun phrase referring to a person or persons was coded for *gender–ostensive labeling* (in which the gender of the person in the book is explicitly commented on [e.g., "That looks like a daddy"]; note that this does not include cases where a gendered noun or pronoun is used to express some other proposition [e.g., "The boy is fixing it" would *not* be considered gender ostensive labeling]), *gender contrast* (in which male and female are contrasted with one another; for example, "only boys [can be a firefighter];" "is this a man or—is this a woman or a man?"), and *gender equality* (in which the speaker explicitly notes that both males and females can engage in a particular activity; e.g., "Anybody could fix a bike, right?;" "Girls can play football, and boys can play football?"). Gender labeling and gender contrasts are explicit means of highlighting gender, whereas gender equality is an explicit means of expressing gender egalitarianism.

We then coded all on-task utterances for those that referred to the _target activity_ depicted in the book (such as chopping wood, feeding a baby, baking cookies, fixing a bike), as opposed to any other sort of content (e.g., what a character in the book was wearing). This was done separately for explicit references (on-task utterances referring to a person) and implicit references (on-task utterances not referring to a person). For all such utterances, we also coded _modality_ (can, should, do/are, like) and _valence_ (positive, negative, or question). For example, consider the following exchange between a mother and her 6-year-old daughter:

> Mother: Do boys play with dolls?
> Child: Um, no.

In this case, both utterances would be coded as referring to the target activity, explicitly in the case of the mother, and implicitly in the case of the child. Both would be coded with modality of "do"; valence would be "question" for the mother and "negative" for the child.

Based on utterance content and valence, along with information about the set-up of the page (i.e., sex of target and consistency), we derived _gender stereotyping_ variables: affirming the gender stereotype (e.g., "'Cause we see daddy take the trash out, don't we?"; "Uh-uh ⟨no⟩, I would get scared if I went so fast" [said by a girl in response to her mother asking if she could be a racecar driver]), negating the gender stereotype ("You can be a sailor" [said to a girl]; "And I can't catch frogs" [said by a boy]), or neutral with regard to the gender stereotype ("Flowers are for girls?"; "Only grown-ups" [can drive trucks]). These gender-typing variables will be important in the analyses below of gender-stereotypical content, and in the examination of discourse patterns between mother and child.

A final set of analyses concerned maternal responses to child stereotyping. For each child utterance that was coded as gender-stereotypical (given the system above), we coded the maternal response into one or more of six categories: affirm (mother provides a positive response or repeats child's statement), negate (mother contradicts the child, or provides gendered information that contradicts the child's statement), question-repeat (mother repeats the child's statement in question form, or affirms what the child says in question form), question-expand (mother provides a question that introduces a new person(s) relating to the target activity), question-why (mother asks why), or other (a catch-all for all other questions, statements, or non-responses).[5] The following are examples of the various coding categories:

- affirm: "Right!"; "Mm-hm."
- negate: "Nngh, I don't know, I don't know how to knit" (in response to child suggesting that mother could knit); "You've

29

exercised to music before" (in response to child saying that he never did aerobics)
- question-repeat: "You can?" (in response to child saying "me"); "A lady?" (in response to child saying "Um, a lady")
- question-expand: "Young girls, old girls?" (in response to child saying "Girls play with dolls"); "Girls can do it too, right?" (in response to child saying that boys can play football)
- question-why: "How come?"; "Why not?"
- other: "What kind of doll is she playing with?"; "How old do you think she is?"

PRELIMINARY RESULTS

Table 6 presents basic descriptive data regarding the amount and types of conversation recorded in these interactions. The data are presented by focus (on-task with reference to a person, on-task with no reference to a person, reading, and off-task). Overall, for both mothers and children, most of the utterances were on-task (ranging from 69% to 82% per age group). We therefore have a sizeable database of mother–child conversations focused on people engaged in gender-stereotypical activities (on average 315 on-task utterances per dyad: 124 child utterances and 191 maternal

TABLE 6

MEAN TOTAL NUMBER OF UTTERANCES AND MEAN PERCENTAGES OF EACH UTTERANCE TYPE, AS A FUNCTION OF SPEAKER AND AGE GROUP

	Mean Total	On-task Person[a]	On-task No-Person[b]	Reading[c]	Off-task[d]
Child					
2 years	172	22%	47%	0%	31%
		(10)	(15)	(0)	(13)
4 years	155	39%	43%	1%	17%
		(15)	(16)	(3)	(8)
6 years	164	40%	36%	12%	12%
		(13)	(16)	(11)	(7)
Mother					
2 years	311	38%	32%	9%	20%
		(10)	(10)	(6)	(8)
4 years	250	45%	28%	13%	13%
		(9)	(10)	(7)	(6)
6 years	226	46%	31%	9%	14%
		(9)	(10)	(6)	(6)

Note.—SDs are in parentheses.
[a]Utterances referring to target activity or book, that include reference to a person. [b]Utterances referring to target activity or book, that do not include reference to a person. [c]Utterances that involve reading text in the book. [d]Utterances that are off-task (not referring to target activity or book) or unintelligible.

30

utterances). This database will be the focus of the core analyses, presented in Chapters III–V.

Meanwhile, a few overarching patterns emerged in this examination of the conversations. Mothers talked more than children and were relatively more likely than children to produce references to a person. Somewhat surprisingly, however, the distribution of mothers' speech did not vary by age of child. Among the children, 2-year-olds were less likely to make references to a person, and were more likely to be off-task or unintelligible, compared to the older children. However, even the 2-year-olds produced on-task utterances over two-thirds of the time. Reading was relatively rare overall, probably due in part to the sparse text. Thus, most of the talk was spontaneous conversation generated by the books, but not simply reading of the books. When reading did occur, it was primarily done by the mothers, though the frequency of reading among children increased markedly at 6 years of age. We now turn to Chapter III, to examine the question of how and in what contexts children and mothers express gender essentialism.

NOTES

2. As can be seen in Table 2, all of the labels used in the picture books were gender-neutral (e.g., "firefighter" rather than "fireman"), with one exception: "seamstress." A potential concern is that this form of the word might imply a female referent and so bias the kinds of talk mothers or children would provide. However, an inspection of the talk regarding this page indicated that only three mothers out of 72 (4%) indicated that "seamstress" is a female-specific word: "A seamstress usually means a girl"; "The men are usually called tailors. I think that there's a different name for them"; "A seamstress, the word seamstress sounds like it's a woman word, but a sewing person—I don't know what you would call them, a sewer." (This mother went on to ask, "Is it OK for men to sew, too?," thereby converting the page to one about "sewers" rather than "seamstresses.") In contrast, most mothers (62% of the sample) defined "seamstress" in a gender-neutral manner (e.g., "A seamstress is somebody who makes dresses and suits and all sorts of things like that. They sew things on a big sewing machine") or skipped the word altogether. Furthermore, over one-third of the mothers either provided an example of a male seamstress (e.g., "That man's a seamstress") or agreed with an example provided by their child. None rejected an example of a male seamstress provided by the child. Therefore, although it would have been ideal to avoid any gender-biased language, in this case we believe that the form of the word did not unduly bias participants toward reporting a female stereotype. This lack of effect is probably due to the relative unfamiliarity of the word and the relative rarity of the -ess feminine ending. If we had used a more familiar word (e.g., "actress") or a more familiar ending (e.g., -man), then the wording effect would more likely have been a serious problem.

3. Two-year-olds received a modified version of the task that older children received. However, unlike the older children, they were not provided with the option of saying that *both* males and females could do an activity. Because the task for 2-year-olds did not permit an examination of flexibility, the data from 2-year-olds on this task will not be considered further.

4. All examples here and throughout were excerpted from the transcripts from this study.

5. This coding focused exclusively on responses to stereotype-affirming utterances (in contrast to stereotype-negating utterances) because they were of greatest theoretical interest. Specifically, we wished to explore the question of how often parents implicitly accept or endorse gender-stereotyping on the part of their children. For this question, maternal responses to stereotype affirmations are most relevant.

III. HOW CHILDREN AND MOTHERS EXPRESS GENDER ESSENTIALISM

The question of how and when children and mothers express gender essentialism is the primary focus of this research project. This issue is addressed in seven sets of analyses, examining: (a) gender-stereotypical content; (b) references to general categories of people, such as "girls" or "race-car drivers" (generic noun phrases); (c) gender-ostensive labeling (e.g., "That's a boy"); (d) gender-naming accuracy and errors; (e) expression of gender relative to other social categories (most notably, age); (f) gender contrasts; and (g) expressions of gender equality. Unless otherwise stated, post hoc t-tests were adjusted using the Bonferroni correction. For ease of exposition, we report only p-values (not t or dfs) for the post-hoc tests.

GENDER-STEREOTYPICAL CONTENT

For those utterances referring to the target activity, a speaker could express one of three attitudes toward the gender-typed content implied: he or she could affirm the gender-stereotype (e.g., "I hate 'em" [boy talking about dolls]), negate the gender-stereotype (e.g., "he can" [man doing aerobics]), or be neutral with respect to the stereotype (e.g., "Have you ever seen anybody knitting before?").

We included both cases where the speaker explicitly mentioned a person or persons (e.g., boys, girls, him, her, they, Mommy, John) as well as cases where the speaker provides content information implicitly, without making reference to a person or persons. Including implicit as well as explicit utterances is important, because there were many occasions, particularly for children, where gender-typed content was conveyed by means of an utterance involving no explicit reference to a person. For example, consider the following exchange between a mother and her son (age 4.6

years; attitude toward gender-stereotypical content appears after each utterance in pointed brackets):

Mother:	Are boys allowed to be ballet dancers? ⟨Neutral⟩
Child:	No. ⟨Affirm⟩
Mother:	Why not?
Child:	No! ⟨Affirm⟩
Mother:	Why not?!
Child:	Because ballet dancers are girls. ⟨Affirm⟩

The child affirms a gender stereotype (ballet dancers are girls, not boys) in three separate statements. However, only the third involved explicit mention of a person or persons. The first two, each a simple use of the word "no," nonetheless powerfully convey important gender-stereotyped content, albeit of implicit nature.

Overall Analyses

Descriptive data concerning stereotype affirmations can be found in Table 7. We conducted a 2 (speaker: mother, child) × 3 (age group: 2, 4, 6) × 2 (child sex: boy, girl) × 3 (attitude: affirm, negate, neutral) × 2 (page type: consistent, inconsistent) ANOVA. Speaker, age group, and child sex were between-subjects variables; attitude and page type were repeated measures variables. The dependent measure was the number of utterances

TABLE 7

DESCRIPTIVE STATISTICS FOR THE MAJOR CODING CATEGORIES: STEREOTYPE AFFIRMATIONS, GENERICS, GENDER-OSTENSIVE LABELING, GENDER CONTRASTS, AND GENDER EQUALITY, AS A FUNCTION OF SPEAKER

	Stereotype				
	Affirmations	Generics	Labeling	Contrasts	Equality
Children					
Mean	28.60	12.17	4.34	0.80	4.84
Median	28.00	4.35	2.65	0.00	0.53
SD	12.41	15.98	5.54	1.66	8.16
Range	3–63	0–63	0–31	0–8	0–33
Mothers					
Mean	9.88	12.31	3.18	1.21	3.15
Median	9.00	8.25	2.17	0.80	1.13
SD	4.57	11.68	3.06	1.73	4.96
Range	2–23	0–46	0–15	0–10	0–28

Note.—Numbers represent the number of instances per 100 on-task utterances.

34

referring to the target activity of a given type, divided by the total number of on-task utterances for that speaker in order to control for total amount of talk. Results indicate a main effect for speaker, $F(1, 132) = 9.32$, $p < .005$, $\eta^2 = .07$, indicating that mothers provided more references to the target activity than children.[6] There was also a main effect for age group, $F(2, 132) = 32.41$, $p < .001$, $\eta^2 = .33$, and a speaker × age group interaction, $F(2, 132) = 3.11$, $p < .05$, $\eta^2 = .045$, indicating that for 2-year-olds, children and mothers made equally many references to the target activity, whereas for 4- and 6-year-olds, children referred to the target activity more often than mothers, $p < .05$.

The remaining effects all involved attitude: a main effect for attitude, $F(2, 264) = 23.78$, $p < .001$, $\eta^2 = .15$, an attitude × speaker interaction, $F(2, 264) = 176.00$, $p < .001$, $\eta^2 = .57$, an attitude × consistency interaction, $F(2, 264) = 101.99$, $p < .001$, $\eta^2 = .44$, and an attitude × speaker × consist- × consistency interaction, $F(4, 264) = 12.82$, $p < .001$, $\eta^2 = .09$. Because the three-way interaction subsumes the lower-order effects, we present the three-way interaction here and in Figure 5. The attitude × speaker × con- × consistency interaction reveals that for mothers, neutral attitudes are much more frequent than either affirmations or negations of gender-stereotypes, $p < .001$, which do not differ from one another. In contrast, for children, affirmations of the stereotypes are most frequent overall, followed by negations, followed by neutral utterances, $ps < .001$. However, this pattern interacts with page type. In the presence of gender-consistent pages of the picture book, speakers (mothers and children) are more likely to affirm than to negate a gender stereotype, $p < .001$, whereas in the presence of gender-inconsistent pages of the picture book, speakers are more likely to negate than to affirm a gender stereotype, $p < .001$. Thus, the nature of the picture book context has a striking effect on the content of both maternal and child speech. In contrast, neutral attitudes are unaffected by page type, and are consistently higher for mothers than for children, $p < .001$.

The effect of page consistency is potentially an important finding, if it means that picture book content can sway how often parents and children express gender stereotypes. However, there is an alternative interpretation that must be addressed. Namely, the consistency effect could merely be an artifact of mothers and children producing utterances that refer to the people depicted in the book (which by definition affirm the gender stereotype on gender-consistent pages, and deny the gender stereotype on gender-inconsistent pages). To examine this question, we analyzed just *generic* utterances, which refer not to any particular individual but the category in general. What we find is that even focusing just on generics (which by definition cannot refer just to the person in the book), the same significant interaction between attitude and consistency arises, where consistent

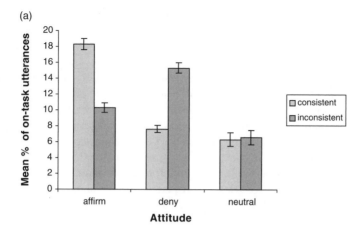

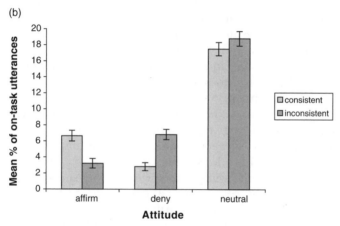

Note: Vertical bars depict standard errors of the means. (a) Children; (b) Mothers.

FIGURE 5.—Mean percentage of on-task utterances that affirm, deny, or are neutral toward gender stereotypes, as a function of speaker and page-type (consistent vs. inconsistent).

pages are associated primarily with affirmations of gender stereotypes (e.g., "Um, boys can" on a page depicting a boy playing with toy trucks), and inconsistent pages are associated primarily with negations of gender stereotypes (e.g., "Boys" in response to "Who can play with dolls?" on a page depicting a boy playing with dolls). (This result is reported in more detail in Chapter IV, examining how generics differ from non-generics.) Thus, the content of the picture book page has a far-reaching impact on mother and child speech.

Overall, then, mothers primarily express *neutral* attitudes about gender stereotypes (often because they are posing questions about them), whereas children primarily *endorse* gender stereotypes, and increasingly so throughout the age range studied here. Follow-up *t*-tests comparing affirmations with negations at each age group revealed that mothers never showed a significant difference between affirmations and negations, whereas children affirmed more than negated the stereotypes at ages 4 and 6 years (*t*-paired(23) = 3.00 and 3.40, *p*s < .01), but not at 2 years of age (*t*-paired(23) = 1.29, *p* > .20). It is important to keep in mind that, if speakers were simply to talk about the information provided in the book, affirmations and denials of stereotypes would be exactly equal. That 4- and 6-year-old children produce more affirmations than denials demonstrates that they are expressing their own beliefs in these conversations. Finally, the information provided in the book (either consistent or inconsistent with the gender stereotype) also plays a powerful role in both child and mother speech.

Analyses Involving Sex of Referent

We were also interested in how these patterns would be distributed as a function of sex-of-referent: that is, would either females or males be discussed in more stereotyped fashion? In order to examine this question, we needed to conduct a separate analysis of just those utterances for which the referent was gendered. (This was necessary because ungendered referents were by definition not categorized as either affirming or negating the stereotype, and thus ungendered referents could not be included as a separate category of analysis.) We therefore conducted an analysis of the same data described above, yet removing those cases of neutral-attitude utterances that used gender-neutral nouns (for example, removing "maybe kids or adults"), but leaving in all stereotype-affirming utterances, all stereotyping-denying utterances, and all stereotype-neutral utterances that involved a gendered referent (for example, keeping in "Does Grandma know how to knit?"). We then conducted a 2 (speaker: mother, child) × 3 (age group: 2, 4, 6) × 2 (child sex: boy, girl) × 3 (attitude: affirm, negate, neutral) × 2 (page type: consistent, inconsistent) × 2 (sex of referent: male, female) ANOVA. The dependent measure was the number of utterances referring to the target activity of a given type, divided by the total number of on-task utterances for that speaker.

Because our interest here is specifically in the effects of sex-of-referent, and in order not to be redundant with the analysis reported above, we report only those significant results involving sex-of-referent. See Figure 6 for results. We found five significant effects involving sex of referent. First, there was a referent-sex × child sex interaction, $F(1, 132) = 154.00$,

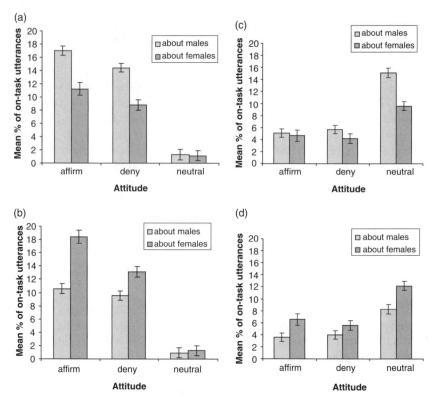

Note: Vertical bars depict standard errors of the means. (a) Boys; (b) Girls; (c) Mothers of Boys; (d) Mothers of Girls.

FIGURE 6.—Mean percentage of on-task utterances that affirm, deny, or are neutral toward gender stereotypes, as a function of sex-of-referent, speaker, and child sex. Numbers reported are averaged across the three age groups.

$p < .001$, $\eta^2 = .54$, indicating that participants talked more about females when the child was a girl, and talked more about males when the child was a boy, $ps < .001$. Next, there was a referent-sex × child sex × speaker interaction, $F(1, 132) = 5.69, p < .02, \eta^2 = .04$, indicating that the above effect was greater for children than for their mothers, although significant for both. We also obtained an attitude × referent-sex interaction, $F(2, 264) = 5.24$, $p < .01$, $\eta^2 = .04$, indicating a small but consistent tendency for speakers to affirm gender stereotypes more frequently when talking about females than when talking about males, $p < .02$. This two-way interaction was subsumed under two higher-order interactions: an attitude × referent-sex × child sex interaction, $F(2, 264) = 4.96$, $p < .01$, $\eta^2 = .04$, and an attitude × referent-sex × child sex × speaker interaction, $F(2, 264) = 39.92$, $p < .001$, $\eta^2 = .23$.

Although 4-way interactions are challenging to interpret, it appears to reflect a tendency for girl participants, and mothers of girls, to carry the effect of the female bias. Girls and mothers of girls affirm stereotypes more for females than males, $p < .01$. In contrast, boys affirm stereotypes more for males than females, $p < .001$, and mothers of boys affirm stereotypes equally often for males and females.

Analyses Involving Valence of Utterance

To this point we have not examined the *valence* of each utterance (namely, whether the utterance expresses a *positive* proposition, a *negative* proposition, or a *question*). Instead, stereotype-affirming utterances were a combination of positive-valence ("Maybe Dad" [can catch frogs]) and negative-valence ("Mans [men] can't knit!") utterances. Likewise, stereotype-negations were a combination of positive-valence ("We do have women firefighters") and negative-valence ("I can't play football" [said by a boy]) utterances. Stereotype-neutral utterances were a combination of all three types of valences (positive: "Football players can play football;" negative: "Babies couldn't really" [paint houses]; questioning: "Do you think she can play hopscotch?"). We were unable to examine valence in the prior analyses because non-neutral attitudes (affirmations and negations) were by definition non-questioning in valence. However, it is also of interest to determine how positive and negative valence utterances differ.

To examine this issue, we conducted an analysis focusing just on positive- and negative-valence utterances, and just those involving gendered referents. (Questioning-valence utterances and gender-neutral referents were excluded so that we could have a balanced design.) Specifically, we conducted a 2 (speaker: mother, child) × 3 (age group: 2, 4, 6) × 2 (child sex: boy, girl) × 3 (attitude: affirm, negate, neutral) × 2 (valence: positive, negative) × 2 (sex of referent: male, female) ANOVA. The dependent measure was the number of utterances referring to the target activity of a given type, divided by the total number of on-task utterances for that speaker.

Because our interest here is specifically in the effects of valence, and in order not to be redundant with the analyses reported above, we report only those significant results involving valence. See Figure 7 for results. As can be seen, there was a powerful main effect of valence, $F(1, 132) = 588.24$, $p < .001$, $\eta^2 = .82$, indicating that positive-valence utterances were much more frequent than negative-valence utterances. However, this main effect was tempered by speaker (valence × speaker interaction, $F(1, 132) = 85.61$, $p < .001$, $\eta^2 = .39$), by age group (valence × age group interaction, $F(2, 132) = 5.52$, $p < .01$, $\eta^2 = .08$), and by child sex (valence × child sex interaction, $F(1, 132) = 5.94$, $p < .02$, $\eta^2 = .04$). As can be seen, children were

39

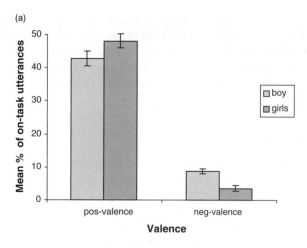

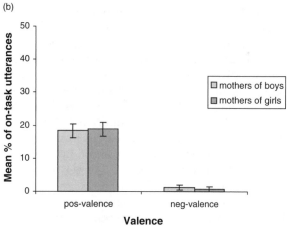

Note: Vertical bars depict standard errors of the means. (a) Children; (b) Mothers.

FIGURE 7.—Mean percentage of on-task utterances regarding gender stereotypes, as a function of valence, speaker, and child sex.

relatively more likely to provide negative-valence utterances than their mothers, and older children were relatively more likely to provide negative-valence utterances than 2-year-olds. The 2-way interaction with child sex needs to be interpreted in light of the 3-way valence × child sex × speaker interaction, $F(1, 132) = 4.16$, $p < .05$, $\eta^2 = .03$. As shown in Figure 7, girls were as likely as boys to provide positive-valence utterances, n.s., whereas boys were more likely than girls to provide negative-valence utterances, $p < .001$. In other words, boys were particularly likely to talk about

40

ways in which people *can't*, *don't*, or *shouldn't* do a particular activity. In contrast, mothers provided equivalent numbers of positive valence utterances to girls and to boys, and they provided equivalent numbers of negative valence utterances to girls and to boys, both comparisons n.s. by Bonferroni.

We obtained an attitude × valence × child sex interaction, $F(1, 132)$ = 4.49, $p < .05$, $\eta^2 = .03$, indicating that positive-valence stereotype affirmations (e.g., "I'm going to do hopscotch" [said by a girl]) were higher in conversations with girls than in conversations with boys, $p = .058$, whereas negative-valence stereotype affirmations (e.g., "Girls can't play football") were higher in conversations with boys than in conversations with girls, $p < .005$. For stereotype negations (e.g., "I don't think [girl's name] does it too much anymore" [play with dolls]), the only significant effect was that negative-valence utterances were more frequent in conversations with boys than in conversations with girls, $p = .01$. This interaction is illustrated in Figure 8.

Finally, there were several interactions involving valence and utterance sex. There was an utterance sex × valence interaction, $F(1, 132) = 5.31$, $p < .05$, $\eta^2 = .04$, indicating that positive-valence talk is slightly more often about females than males (e.g., "Grandma can sew"), whereas negative-valence talk is slightly more often about males than females (e.g., "No" in response to, "Can boys?"), although neither comparison reaches statistical significance. There was also an utterance sex × valence × child sex interaction, $F(1, 132) = 53.08$, $p < .001$, $\eta^2 = .29$, indicating that the above effect was modulated by child sex, since conversations with girls overall were more about females than males, and conversations with boys overall were more about males than females. This interaction is illustrated in Figure 9. Finally, there was an utterance sex × valence × child sex × speaker interaction, $F(1, 132) = 9.20$, $p < .005$, $\eta^2 = .065$. Although difficult to interpret, this seems to reflect the fact that the above effects are clearer with children than with mothers, who produced fewer utterances overall, and especially few negative-valence utterances.

The remaining two interactions also involved speaker attitude (i.e., either stereotype-affirming or stereotype-denying). There was an attitude × utterance sex × valence interaction, $F(1, 132) = 12.95$, $p < .001$, $\eta^2 = .09$. What we see is that the tendency for speakers to endorse stereotypes about females more than about males (discussed above in the section on sex-of-referent) was carried by positive-valence utterances, $p < .001$, not negative-valence utterances, n.s. See Figure 10. Finally, there was a four-way interaction involving attitude, utterance sex, valence, and age group, $F(2, 132) = 3.89$, $p < .05$, $\eta^2 = .06$. This interaction indicates that the effect described above is present in conversations with 4- and 6-year-olds, $ps < .005$, but not in conversations with 2-year-olds, n.s.

(a)

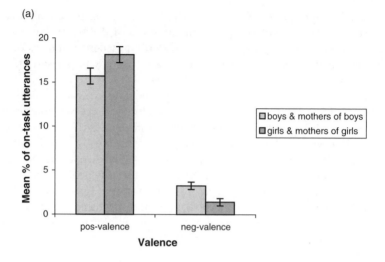

(b)

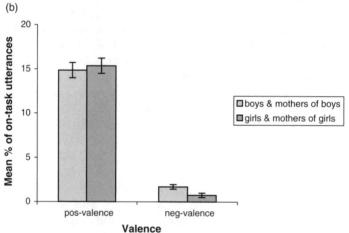

Note: Vertical bars depict standard errors of the means. (a) Stereotype affirmations ("She's a ballerina"; "Grandma can't [chop wood]"); (b) Stereotype negations ("My dad knows how to sew"; "You don't like to touch frogs" [said by mother to son]).

FIGURE 8.—Mean percentage of on-task utterances regarding gender stereotypes, as a function of attitude, valence, and child sex.

GENERIC NOUN PHRASES

Generic noun phrases refer to a category as a whole (e.g., "*Boys* don't ever be ballet dancers;" "*Girls*. Never. Play. With. That. Never do."). They

(a)

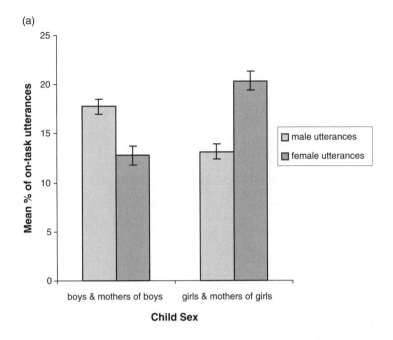

(b)

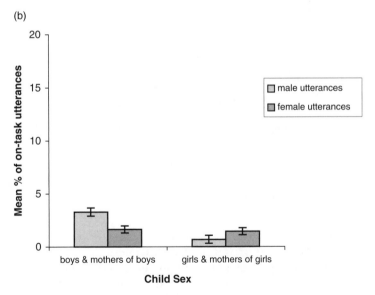

Note: Vertical bars depict standard errors of the means. (a) Positive-valence utterances; (b) Negative-valence utterances.

FIGURE 9.—Mean percentage of on-task utterances regarding gender stereotypes, as a function of sex-of-referent, valence, and child sex.

43

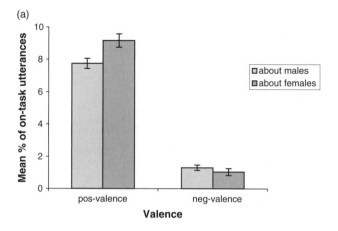

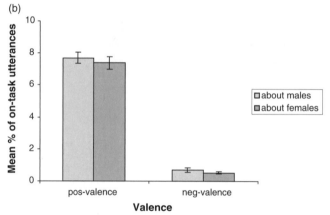

Note: Vertical bars depict standard errors of the means. (a) Stereotype affirmations ("She's a ballerina"; "Grandma can't [chop wood]"); (b) Stereotype negations ("My dad knows how to sew"; "You don't like to touch frogs" [said by mother to son]).

FIGURE 10.—Mean percentage of on-task utterances regarding gender stereotypes, as a function of attitude, sex-of-referent, and valence.

can be distinguished from *individual* reference (e.g., "Do you know, I had a roommate in college that played football"). Generics therefore provide a means of emphasizing a category without necessarily making explicitly gender-stereotyped statements. Indeed, an utterance can be neutral or even denying of a gender stereotype, while still implying that gender is an appropriate basis on which to make generalizations (e.g., "Can girls deliver newspapers?"; "I think boys can help bake cookies, too"). It is thus important to determine when children hear generics, and when they produce them. All analyses in this section focus exclusively on those utterances in which a speaker made explicit reference to the generic category using a noun or pronoun (thereby excluding cases where there was no person reference; e.g., excluding utterances such as "Yeah" in reply to, "Can dads knit sweaters?"). Overall descriptive data concerning generics can be found in Table 7.

We analyzed generics that referred in any way to the target activity (which accounted for the bulk of generics). The primary analysis was a 2 (speaker: mother, child) $\times$ 3 (age group: 2, 4, 6) $\times$ 2 (child sex: boy, girl) $\times$ 2 (page type: consistent, inconsistent) $\times$ 2 (sex of referent: male, female, other) ANOVA. The dependent measure was the number of generic utterances referring to the target activity of a given type, divided by the total number of on-task utterances for that speaker.

Several important findings emerged. There was a main effect of age group, $F(2, 132) = 23.16$, $p < .001$, $\eta^2 = .26$, indicating that generics increased markedly with child age, from 2.91 to 14.05 to 19.75 ($SDs = 4.07$, 13.33, and 15.75) at ages 2, 4, and 6, respectively (see Figure 11a). This increase was significant between 2 and 4 years of age, for both children and mothers, $ps < .01$, and between 4 and 6 years of age for children, $p < .05$, though not significantly different between 4 and 6 years for mothers. There was a consistency $\times$ speaker interaction, $F(1, 132) = 7.23$, $p < .01$, $\eta^2 = .05$, indicating that mothers produced generics more for gender-inconsistent pages than for gender-consistent pages ($M = 7.05$ and 5.26, $SD = 6.87$ and 5.41), $p < .01$, whereas children produced generics equally for the two page types ($M = 5.85$ and 6.32, $SD = 7.77$ and 9.18).

The remaining significant effects all involved referent sex: referent sex $\times$ age group, $F(4, 264) = 4.34$, $p < .005$, $\eta^2 = .06$, referent sex $\times$ child sex, $F(2, 264) = 4.71$, $p = .01$, $\eta^2 = .03$, and referent sex $\times$ speaker, $F(2, 264) = 6.63$, $p < .005$, $\eta^2 = .05$. We illustrate these interactions in Figures 11b–d. As the figures illustrate, there were systematic effects involving gender-neutral generics (those involving categories such as "firefighters," "children," or "grown-ups"). First, generics to and from girls were more likely to be gender-neutral than generics to and from boys, $p < .01$. Second, mothers' generics were more likely to be gender-neutral than children's generics, $p = .01$. Third, whereas both 2- and 4-year-olds produced gender-neutral generics, male generics, and female generics in equal numbers, 6-year-olds produced male generics more than either female generics or neutral generics, both $ps < .01$. To frame this somewhat differently: boys, children, and 6-year-olds were relatively more focused on gender, in their generics.

The interactions with referent sex also indicated that dyads produced more generics about male targets than about female targets, although this tendency increased with age (significant male–female difference among conversations with 6-year-olds only, as reported above), was more

45

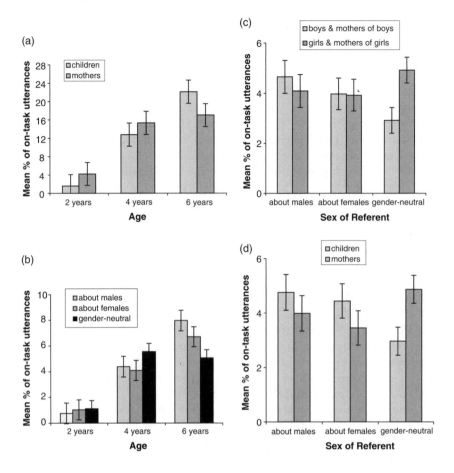

Note: Vertical bars depict standard errors of the means. (a) As a function of speaker and age group; (b) As a function of sex-of-referent and age group; (c) As a function of sex-of-referent and child sex; (d) As a function of sex-of-referent and speaker.

FIGURE 11.—Generics as a mean percentage of on-task utterances.

powerful in speech to and from boys than in speech to and from girls (significant male–female difference among conversations with boys only, $p < .05$), and was more powerful among mothers than among children.

GENDER-OSTENSIVE LABELING

Gender-ostensive labeling entails direct mention of the gender of a character in the picture book, in an utterance that conveys no other content.

For example, "A man," "That's a girl," "Is that a he or a she?," or "That looks like a daddy" would all be counted as gender-ostensive labeling.[7] In contrast, other statements that make reference to a character's sex, but in the context of providing other information, would not count as gender-ostensive labeling (e.g., "This boy is fixing it"). (Such references will be analyzed later, in the section entitled, "Gender vs. Other Categories.") Thus, the point of gender-ostensive labeling is to convey gender information. We find these of theoretical interest because they mark a speaker's attention to gender per se. At times the dyads would engage in rather lengthy discussions of the gender of a particular person in the book. For example, consider the following excerpt of a mother and her son (age 2.5 years), talking about a girl playing football (lines coded as gender-ostensive labeling are indicated below in pointed brackets):

Mother:	Who is that playing football?
Child:	Da.
Mother:	Who is that?
Child:	Who is dat?
Child:	Gir. [sic]
Mother:	Girl? ⟨Label⟩
Child:	A man? ⟨Label⟩
Mother:	Or a man? ⟨Label⟩
Child:	A man. ⟨Label⟩
Child:	Girl. ⟨Label⟩
Mother:	A woman? ⟨Label⟩
Child:	(No), a girl. ⟨Label⟩
Mother:	A girl. ⟨Label⟩
Mother:	She's playing football, huh?
Child:	She's playing foot, ball.

Overall descriptive data for gender-ostensive labeling appear in Table 7. To examine the contexts in which gender-ostensive labeling takes place, we conducted a 3 (age: 2, 4, 6) × 2 (child sex: boy, girl) × 2 (speaker: child, mother) × 2 (sex of referent: male, female) × 2 (page type: consistent, inconsistent) ANOVA. The dependent measure was the number of gender-ostensive labeling statements, divided by the total number of on-task utterances for that speaker. There was a main effect of age, $F(2, 132) = 3.55$, $p < .05$, $\eta^2 = .05$, indicating that gender-ostensive labeling was higher in conversations with 2-year-olds ($M = 5.06$) than in conversations with 4-year-olds ($M = 2.66$), $p < .05$. Gender-ostensive labeling was intermediate in frequency among conversations with 6-year-olds ($M = 3.57$), and not significantly different from the other two age groups.

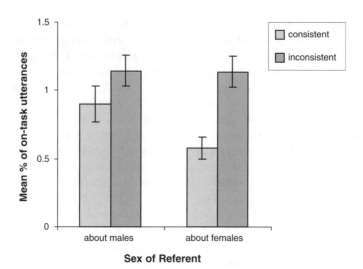

Note: Vertical bars depict standard errors of the means.

FIGURE 12.—Gender-ostensive labeling as a mean percentage of on-task utterances, as a function of sex-of-referent and page consistency.

There was also a main effect of sex of referent, $F(1, 132) = 4.23$, $p < .05$, $\eta^2 = .03$, a main effect of consistency, $F(1, 132) = 36.72$, $p < .001$, $\eta^2 = .22$, and a sex-of-referent × consistency interaction, $F(1, 132) = 5.07$, $p < .05$, $\eta^2 = .03$. Gender-ostensive labeling was higher in reference to males than to females ($M = 2.05$ and 1.71, $SDs = 2.64$ and 2.23), and was higher in reference to inconsistent pages in the picture book (e.g., a woman race-car driver) than to consistent pages in the picture book (e.g., a woman feeding a baby) ($M = 2.28$ and 1.48, $SDs = 2.40$ and 2.36). However, the male advantage was found on gender-consistent pages only, $p < .005$. See Figure 12.

GENDER NAMING ACCURACY AND ERRORS

Naming Accuracy and Errors Overall

We next examine children's accuracy and errors in naming the gender of pictures in the picture books. Naming accuracy reveals children's sensitivity to gender, specifically, whether they can identify gender on the basis of appearance cues. Naming errors are potentially valuable as an implicit measure of gender stereotyping. Specifically, if children are knowledgeable about gender stereotypes, then we should expect more naming errors on stereotype-inconsistent pages (e.g., woman firefighter) than on stereotype-

48

consistent pages (e.g., man firefighter). Past researchers have found that school-aged children show better memory for gender-consistent information, and distortion of counter-stereotypic information (e.g., Bigler & Liben, 1990; Cordua, McGraw, & Drabman, 1979; Koblinsky, Cruse, & Sugawara, 1978; Liben & Signorella, 1980; Martin & Halverson, 1983; Signorella & Liben, 1984; Stangor & Ruble, 1989), although we are unaware of past work examining naming errors as an index of stereotype knowledge. Both accuracy and errors are of particular interest with children of the youngest age studied here, given the sharp increase with age in children's stereotype affirmations and generics. Children's naming errors provide an indirect and potentially more sensitive means of assessing the youngest children's attention to gender.

We wish to make clear how the naming accuracy and errors in this section differ from the *Gender-ostensive labeling* section above, which also examines naming. Whereas the gender-ostensive labeling section focused exclusively on those statements whose function is solely to provide a label (e.g., "A lady"; "That's the mama!"), children's naming examined in this section entails all references to the pictures in the book (including, for example, "He can"; "She has yellow and she has blue"). Furthermore, whereas the gender-ostensive labeling section focused exclusively on the referent (e.g., did the labeling statement refer to a male or a female?), this naming section examines the *accuracy* of the reference.

To analyze these data, we examined all of children's references to the pictures in the picture book. References that involved pointing only (with no accompanying language) were excluded from consideration. Each reference was coded in one of three ways: correct gender form (e.g., "He" to refer to a boy catching frogs); incorrect gender form (e.g., "A man" to refer to a girl playing football); or neutral with respect to gender (e.g., "That's a grown-up" to refer to a boy fixing a bicycle). Altogether there were 954 references, with an average of 18.00 at age 2 years, 11.00 at age 4 years, and 10.75 at age 6 years. A preliminary repeated measures ANOVA (2: consistency × 3: age group) indicated that there were more references overall to inconsistent than consistent pages, $F(1,66) = 8.54$, $p < .01$, $\eta^2 = .11$. Furthermore, the total number of references to pictures in the book significantly decreased with age, $F(2,66) = 3.36$, $p < .05$, $\eta^2 = .09$.

Given the baseline differences between consistent and inconsistent pages, we calculated each participant's scores as a percent of all his or her references, for consistent and inconsistent pages separately. That is, for each speaker, all references for a given page type (consistent vs. inconsistent) were summed, and we examined correct, incorrect, and neutral responses as a percentage of that participant's total references for that type. We then conducted three separate repeated measures ANOVAs, one for each of

TABLE 8

MEAN PERCENTAGE CORRECT, INCORRECT, AND GENDER-NEUTRAL NAMING OF PICTURES IN
PICTURE BOOKS, AS A FUNCTION OF PAGE CONSISTENCY AND AGE GROUP (CHILDREN ONLY)

	2 years	4 years	6 years
Correct			
Consistent	83 (17)	86 (26)	88 (21)
Inconsistent	76 (16)	92 (10)	81 (28)
Incorrect			
Consistent	5 (7)	4 (13)	1 (5)
Inconsistent	16 (10)	4 (6)	7 (21)
Neutral			
Consistent	11 (15)	9 (16)	11 (21)
Inconsistent	8 (13)	4 (6)	12 (23)

Note.—SDs are in parentheses.

the three dependent measures (correct, incorrect, neutral). Each analysis
was a 3 (age group) × 2 (child sex) × 2 (consistency) ANOVA, with consistency as the repeated-measures variable, and age group and child sex as
between-subjects variables. Three 2-year-olds, eight 4-year-olds, and two 6-
year-olds produced no labels for either consistent pages only, inconsistent
pages only, or both page types, and therefore could not be included in the
analyses.

Results are shown in Table 8. The first point to notice is that the vast
majority of children's references were gendered. Although it was possible to
refer to the pictures using non-gendered language (e.g., that person; the
kid; this one), children spontaneously produced gendered references over
90% of the time. The second point to notice is that children in all three age
groups were highly accurate in identifying the intended gender of the
people in the books. Even the 2-year-olds were correct 79.5% of the time,
and this increased slightly (though non-significantly) to 89% correct at age
4, and 85% correct at age 6. Furthermore, children's naming often occurred
before the mother labeled or referred to the target picture in any gendered
way, therefore indicating that children came up with appropriate gender
classifications by themselves. This high level of performance suggests that
young children were aware of the relevance of the cues provided in the
pictures (primarily differences in hair length and clothing) for determining
gender.

Nonetheless, the third point to notice is that children did make naming
errors, and that page-type (stereotype-consistent vs. -inconsistent) was
associated with different levels of children's accuracy. Specifically, naming
errors were significantly more frequent on stereotype-inconsistent trials
than on stereotype-consistent trials, $F(1, 53) = 6.43$, $p < .02$, $\eta^2 = .11$. This

main effect did not interact with age. However, post hoc tests conducted within each age group revealed that the consistency effect was significant among 2-year-olds only, by paired t-test, $p < .01$. None of the other main effects or interactions were significant. The example below illustrates that children were at times quite firm in their mis-labeling (child is a girl, age 2.94; the picture is of a boy playing with dolls; naming errors are marked in pointy brackets):

Mother: "Who can play with dolls?"
Child: She can. ⟨Naming error⟩
Mother: Is that a she or a he?
Child: She can. ⟨Naming error⟩
Mother: That's a he, isn't it, I think?
Child: She. ⟨Naming error⟩
Mother: You think it's a she?
Child: She. ⟨Naming error⟩
Mother: You do?
Mother: Maybe.

Naming Accuracy and Errors as a Function of Gender Cues in the Pictures

Finally, we examined how children's gender-stereotyping naming errors corresponded to the number of gender cues available in the pictures. We predicted that children would make more naming errors on pictures displaying fewer gender cues. In order to conduct this analysis, we first compared the two versions of each activity (e.g., man chopping wood vs. woman chopping wood) and counted how many of the following five dimensions differentiated the two: hair on head (e.g., short hair for male, long hair for female); facial hair (moustache or beard for male); hair decorations (ribbon, bow, or barrette for female); clothing type (e.g., skirt for female, tie for male); clothing color or pattern (e.g., pink outfit or flowered blouse for female). We designed the pictures so that each picture-pair would differ on at least one dimension. The higher the score, the more sex-differentiated are the pictures. However, the number of cues necessarily ranged, because in some cases either a full view of the character wasn't possible (e.g., truck driver) or a unisex uniform was depicted (e.g., firefighter).

On average, the pictures in a pair differed by 2.67 cues ($SD = 0.96$), with a range of 1–4. This indicates that the pictures did appropriately depict male–female differences, as intended, though individual picture-pairs differed in how different the male and female pictures were. For example, the man and woman house-painters differed by only one cue, hair length, whereas the man and woman wood-choppers differed by four cues: hair length, facial hair, clothing type (skirt on the woman, suspenders on the man), and clothing pattern (flowered blouse for woman, solid red shirt for man). We conducted a Pearson correlation between the number of gender cues in a picture pair and the number of stereotype-consistent labeling errors by 2-year-olds for that pair. As predicted, there was a significant negative correlation, $-.46$ ($N = 24$), $p < .05$, indicating that pictures that had relatively fewer gender cues received relatively more labeling errors.

Thus, children were sensitive to the amount of gendered information in the picture, in their labeling. However, number of cues per se could not fully account for the number of labeling errors. When we looked at each picture in a pair separately, we found that pictures of females typically had more visible gendered cues than pictures of males ($M = 2.33$ and 1.29, $SD = 0.96$ and 0.46, respectively; $p < .01$ by binomial test), yet children made more naming errors in the direction of the stereotype in response to female pictures than to male pictures ($M = 1.08$ and 0.54, $SD = 1.32$ and 0.98, respectively; $p < .05$ by binomial test). In other words, despite the greater availability of gender-specific cues in the female pictures, they were associated with more errors. (The greater availability of gender-specific cues in the female pictures reflects cultural differences in Western attire for males and females: a greater variety of clothing and decorations are female-specific than male-specific. Consider, for example, that dresses, skirts, hair decorations, and pink fabrics are female-specific, whereas pants, hats, and blue fabrics could be either male or female.) Moreover, the finding presented earlier, that gender-inconsistent pages led to more errors than gender-consistent pages, resulted despite the fact that the amount of gender cues for the two sorts of pages did not significantly differ ($M = 1.62$ and 2.00, $SD = 0.82$ and 0.98, respectively; $p > .40$ by binomial test).

These results therefore suggest that visual cues are related to children's naming errors, but that other factors are also important, including consistency with a gender stereotype, and gender of the person in the picture. These latter cues reflect children's knowledge and conceptual beliefs concerning gender and gender stereotypes.

Summary

An analysis of children's naming accuracy and errors, focusing on their references to the people depicted in the picture books, reveals three primary findings. First, children spontaneously used gendered language to make reference to the people in the picture books. Despite the fact that these were unfamiliar people, children as young as 2 years of age did not hesitate to classify them as male or female, over 90% of the time that they did make reference to a person. Second, children were highly accurate in identifying the intended gender of the people in the book. Despite the relative lack of detail in the pictures, and despite the fact that the activities mismatched gender stereotypes on half the pages, children were highly accurate in their labeling. Children typically did use the correctly gendered form, whether that was a noun, pronoun, or proper name. Even 2-year-olds were correct nearly 80% of the time. Third, and especially important, 2-year-olds made more errors on gender-inconsistent pages than on gender-consistent pages. Specifically, their naming errors are biased to show *conformity* with the gender stereotype. This indicates that the 2-year-olds in this study are aware of gender stereotypes at some level; otherwise, there would be no reason for them to make errors more on one type of page than another. Two-year-olds' gender stereotype knowledge appears to influence their expectations and interpretations of what they see in the books.

Although past work has documented better memory for stereotypic than counter-stereotypic information and more distortion of counter-stereotypic than stereotypic information (see Martin, Ruble, & Szkrybalo, 2002; Signorella, Bigler, & Liben, 1997), these data are new in two respects. First, they show a similar effect on a labeling task, that does not impose any memory load whatsoever. And second, they demonstrate an effect at an earlier age than most past research, namely, in 2-year-old children. Thus, children's picture naming can be used as a subtle means of assessing very early knowledge of gender stereotypes.

REFERENCES TO GENDER VS. OTHER CATEGORIES

Gender vs. Age

How often do children and their mothers focus on gender relative to other categories? We examined this question by analyzing all on-task references to a person, including nouns (e.g., boy, girl, cheerleader, kid, person), pronouns (e.g., he, she, I, you, they), proper nouns (e.g., Alex, Kayla, Daddy), and other (e.g., anyone, who, this). (This analysis differs from the section entitled *Gender Naming Accuracy and Errors*, above, which focused exclusively on children's references to pictures in the picture book. In contrast, the present analysis examines all person-references, including those of people not depicted in the book.) In each case, we examined whether the form of reference made explicit mention of gender (see distinction between content and form in the coding scheme, Table 2). As a basis of comparison, we also examined whether the form of reference made explicit mention of age. Age was selected a dimension for several reasons. First, it is a highly important social category that is salient to children as well as adults (Taylor & Gelman, 1993). Second, each picture in the book explicitly depicted a person of an identifiable gender and age group. Third, across the entire book, the pictures were balanced across both gender (half male, half female) and age (half adult, half child), with a perfect crossing of these two factors.

53

TABLE 9

MEAN PROPORTION OF PERSON REFERENCES THAT MARKED GENDER AND AGE, RESPECTIVELY,
AS A FUNCTION OF WORD TYPE (NOUNS; PRONOUNS, AND PROPER NOUNS; OTHER)

	Overall	Nouns	Pronouns/ Proper Nouns	Other
Children				
Gender	.54 (.23)	.74 (.24)	.44 (.24)	.00 (.00)
Age	.36 (.23)	.81 (.20)	.11 (.10)	.00 (.00)
Mothers				
Gender	.47 (.13)	.61 (.19)	.55 (.17)	.00 (.00)
Age	.24 (.11)	.65 (.18)	.08 (.06)	.00 (.00)

Note.—SDs are in parentheses.

In examining age vs. gender references, the different word forms need to be considered separately, because they differ in what is expressible in English. For example, pronouns in English (e.g., he, she, it) often encode gender but never encode age. In contrast, English has a variety of nouns that encode age only (e.g., kid, toddler, infant, preschooler, 2-year-old, senior, grown-up, teenager, baby, child, adult, old person), but only a few nouns that exclusively encode gender (sister, brother, male, female). Because there were relatively few proper nouns, and because proper nouns pattern primarily like pronouns (more likely to encode gender than age), we collapsed pronouns and proper nouns into a single group.

Table 9 displays the mean proportion of person references that marked gender and age, respectively, as a function of word type (nouns; pronouns and proper nouns; other). As can be seen, gender was marked more often than age overall, though this varied markedly by word type. Proper nouns and pronouns often marked gender but rarely marked age, due to limitations of the English language (where only names for family members mark age; e.g., "Mommy"). References in the "other" category never marked gender or age, again due to limitations of the English language. With nouns, the percentages are similar overall (68% marking gender; 74% marking age), indicating greater choice in expression.

Analysis of Nouns Only

The nouns are of greatest interest because they permit more choice by the speaker. We conducted a 2 (speaker: mother, child) × 3 (age group: 2, 4, 6) × 2 (child sex: boy, girl) × 2 (dimension: gender, age) repeated measures ANOVA, with dimension as the repeated-measures variable, and speaker, age group, and child sex as between-subjects variables. The dependent measure was the proportion of nouns marking gender or age,

TABLE 10

Mean Proportion of Person-Referring Nouns Marked for Gender, Age, Gender and Age, or Neither Gender nor Age

	Gender	Age	Gender+Age	Neither
Children	.01 (.05)	.08 (.15)	.74 (.23)	.16 (.19)
Mothers	.01 (.02)	.06 (.09)	.60 (.19)	.33 (.18)

Note.—SDs are in parentheses.

respectively. These results yielded a main effect of dimension, $F(1, 128) = 24.50, p < .001, \eta^2 = .16$, indicating that age was marked slightly more often than gender. However, this effect was moderated by age group, in a dimension × age group interaction, $F(2, 128) = 8.73, p < .001, \eta^2 = .12$. For 2-year-olds, gender and age were expressed equally often, whereas for both 4-year-olds and 6-year-olds, age was expressed more than gender. Finally, there was a main effect of speaker, $F(1, 128) = 26.56, p < .001, \eta^2 = .17$, indicating that children marked both gender and age more than their mothers.

We next conducted a more detailed analysis of noun references, to determine how often speakers refer to social categories *other than* gender or age. For each participant, we tallied the number of on-task person references that explicitly marked gender only, age only, both gender and age, or neither gender nor age. We then normalized these scores by dividing by the total number of on-task utterances for each speaker, and multiplying by 100. As can be seen in Table 10, the vast majority of person-references involving a noun expressed both gender and age (70%); an additional 9% expressed either age only (8%) or gender only (1%). Only 20% of person-references involving a noun expressed neither gender nor age. These included a variety of categories, most commonly non-specific reference to people (person, people) and occupation terms (cheerleader, firefighter, race-car driver, sailor), but also occasionally any of a range of other categories ("a truck guy," "campers").

Summary

Gender was commonly expressed by both children and their mothers in this dataset. Roughly half the time that a reference was made to a person, it included explicit mention of the person's gender. Gender was expressed much more often than age (nearly twice as often, in mothers' speech). To some extent this is a function of the expressive capabilities of the English language (e.g., many pronouns and proper nouns obligatorily express gender; few proper nouns and no pronouns can express age). However, even when we focus on nouns, for which speakers have the choice of labeling gender or not (e.g., a speaker could say "kid" instead of "boy"), we find that both children and parents expressed gender over half the time. This is roughly comparable to the frequency with which speakers used nouns to refer to age, and much more common than references to other social categories (such as race, ethnicity, or occupation). We conclude that speakers emphasize gender in their selection of nouns that refer to people.

GENDER CONTRASTS

Gender contrasts involve explicitly contrasting the two genders against one another, for example, "That's for girls only," "Is that a girl job or a boy job?," "That's for girls, not boys," "Is that a girl or a boy?". They can be considered an implicit means of stereotyping, by implying a binary opposition between males and females: an activity is for one sex only, or a person can be classified as either one sex or the other. Overall descriptive data on gender contrasts appear in Table 7.

To analyze gender contrasts, we conducted a 3 (age: 2, 4, 6) × 2 (child sex: boy, girl) × 2 (speaker: child, mother) × 2 (sex of referent: male, female) × 2 (page type: consistent, inconsistent) ANOVA. The dependent measure was the number of gender contrast statements, divided by the total number of on-task utterances for that speaker. See Figure 13 for results. There was a main effect for age group, $F(2, 132) = 4.07$, $p < .02$, $\eta^2 = .06$, indicating increasing gender contrasts from ages 2 to 4 to 6, although only the 2- and 6-year-old groups are significantly different from one another, $p < .02$. There was also a main effect of consistency, $F(1, 132) = 8.55$, $p < .005$, $\eta^2 = .06$, a consistency × speaker interaction, $F(1, 132) = 4.20$, $p < .05$, $\eta^2 = .03$, and a consistency × age group interaction, $F(2, 132) = 4.43$, $p < .02$, $\eta^2 = .06$. These results indicate that gender-contrasts were more frequent in reference to gender-inconsistent pages (e.g., man doing ballet) than to gender-consistent pages (man chopping wood). However, this page-consistency effect was significant among mothers only, $p = .001$, not children, and was significant in conversations with 6-year-olds only, $p < .001$, and not in conversations with the younger children.

EXPRESSIONS OF GENDER EQUALITY

In addition to examining explicit and implicit mention of gender stereotyping, we also examined expressions of gender equality. This entailed direct statements of the following sort: "Anyone can do it," "Both boys and girls can do it," "Boys and girls," "Either," "Men and women," "Boys can do

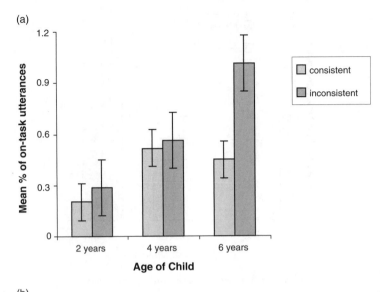

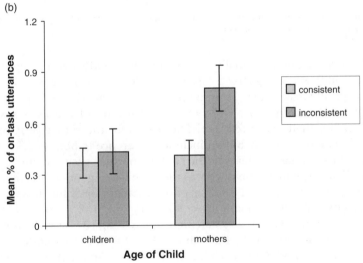

Note: Vertical bars depict standard errors of the means. (a) As a function of page consistency and age group; (b) As a function of page consistency and speaker.

FIGURE 13.—Gender contrasts as a mean percentage of on-task utterances.

it, too," or "Usually girls, but sometimes boys." These are important because they express the opposite of gender stereotyping, which were the focus of the earlier analyses. Overall descriptive data on gender equality are presented in Table 7.

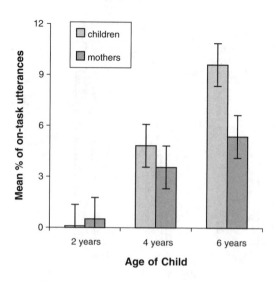

Note: Vertical bars depict standard errors of the means.

FIGURE 14.—Gender equality statements as a mean percentage of on-task utterances, as a function of age group and speaker.

To analyze gender equality statements, we conducted a 3 (age: 2, 4, 6) × 2 (child sex: boy, girl) × 2 (speaker: child, mother) × 2 (activity sex:[8] stereotypically male activity, stereotypically female activity) × 2 (page type: consistent, inconsistent) ANOVA. (Note that we included activity sex as a factor, rather than sex-of-referent. The reason for this is that most gender equality statements by definition included reference to both males and females. Thus of greater interest is the context in which such statements were made.) The dependent measure was the number of gender equality statements, divided by the total number of on-task utterances for that speaker.

Results indicated a main effect for age, $F(2, 132) = 16.40$, $p < .001$, $\eta^2 = .20$, with gender equality statements increasing consistently from 2 to 4–6 years of age ($M = 0.30$, 4.20, and 7.49, $SD = 0.62$, 6.07, and 8.73, respectively), for mothers and children combined. Although there was no significant age × speaker interaction, we examined the age effect separately for children and mothers, to determine if the increase holds among both groups (see Figure 14). That is, we did not wish to assume that age was significant for *both* children and mothers, simply on the basis of the interaction failing to reach significance. Children's equality statements increased steadily from 2 to 4–6 years of age, all pairwise comparisons significant at $p < .05$. For mothers, the increase was significant when comparing mothers of 2-year-olds to mothers of 6-year-olds only, $p < .05$. There was also a main effect for page consistency, $F(1, 132) = 5.27$, $p < .05$, $\eta^2 = .04$, indicating that

TABLE 11

PROPORTION OF UTTERANCES THAT RECEIVED OVERLAPPING CODES, AS A FUNCTION OF
CODING CATEGORY

	Generics	Ostensive label	Contrast	Equality
GENERICS	—	.00	.07	.15
OSTENS.LABEL	.01	—	.08	.01
CONTRAST	.53	.21	—	.02
EQUALITY	.41	.01	.01	—

Note.—These scores were derived by dividing a numerator (number of utterances that received overlapping scores for two particular codes) with a denominator (number of total utterances for one of the two codes). In this table, the left-most column (with words in capital letters) indicates the denominator, and the top-most row (with words in lower-case letters) indicates the numerator. For example, the cell with the score of .53 was calculated as the number of utterances that were coded as *both* generic and contrast, divided by the total number of utterances scored as contrast.

expressions of gender equality were more frequent in reference to inconsistent pages in the picture book (e.g., a woman race-car driver) than to consistent pages in the picture book (e.g., a woman feeding a baby); $M = 2.16$ and 1.84, $SD = 3.72$ and 3.24, respectively.

OVERLAP BETWEEN CODING CATEGORIES

Mothers' and children's utterances were multiply coded (e.g., for focus, for scope, for content, etc.). Although each level of coding was conducted independently, an important question concerns the degree of overlap between the various coding categories. For example, when stating a gender contrast, participants may often phrase it generically. To examine this question, we selected the four main types of implicit references (generics, gender-ostensive labeling, gender contrast, and gender equality), cross-tabulated the different categories with one another, then calculated the percentage of each category that was cross-coded with the other. The results can be found in Table 11.

As can be seen, all cells are relatively low (under 25%), with the exception of two: for both gender contrasts and gender equality, a high proportion of the utterances were also double-coded as generic (roughly half). Thus, participants often state gender contrasts in generic form (e.g., "That's for girls, not for boys"), and often state gender equality in generic form (e.g., "Both boys and girls can do it"). Apart from these two cells, the remainder of the codes were fairly independent of one another, indicating that the multiple coding scheme did not simply reflect different ways of expressing the same utterances, but was capturing distinct utterances.

Although complex, the results in this chapter offer a number of systematic generalizations. Consider first expressions of attitudes regarding gender stereotypes, which can be understood as the most explicit form of stereotyping expression. By four years of age, children typically *affirmed* gender stereotypes in their conversations. That is, even though the book depicted examples that negated stereotypes as often as they affirmed stereotypes, in their own talk children typically affirmed gender stereotypes. Interestingly, 2-year-olds did not yet show any consistent tendency to affirm more than negate, but 4- and 6-year-olds did. There may thus be an important developmental change taking place between 2 and 4 years of age, either in children's knowledge of gender stereotypes, or in their willingness to endorse them.

In contrast to their children, mothers did not show any tendency to express stereotype-consistent attitudes in an explicit way. They negated stereotypes as often as they affirmed them, and most often expressed stereotype-neutral attitudes, typically in the form of questions. An interesting point here is that the stereotyping displayed by children in the book-reading task cannot be due simply to modeling or repeating what mothers say in the task, given the mother-child differences obtained. However, this difference raises the question of where children acquired the stereotypes, given mothers' failure to affirm gender stereotypes more than deny them, on this task. One possibility is that children acquire these stereotypes from sources other than the mother alone. Certainly the child's father, siblings, peers (in daycare or the neighborhood), and teachers are all important socializing influences. Likewise, various media (movies, TV programs, books, music) provide extensive information about the social world. Another plausible explanation is that mothers appeared more gender-neutral on this task than they might ordinarily, due to the counter-stereotypical examples provided in the picture books. When we look just at stereotype-consistent pages in the book, then we find that mothers affirm gender stereotypes significantly more than they negate them, at all three ages. (The same is true for children.) It is only on the gender-*inconsistent* pages that mothers show a different pattern. Thus, if we presume that the world typically presents gender-stereotypical content (both in reality and in the media, including books), then overall mothers will be affirming gender stereotypes more than negating them. Finally, social desirability effects may have resulted in less overt gender stereotyping than mothers would ordinarily display.

What about more implicit means of referring to gender? In addition to explicit endorsements of gender stereotypes, both mothers and children used several means of referring to gender using more implicit means, including generics (e.g., Boys are good at football), gender-ostensive labeling (e.g., That's a boy), gender contrasts (e.g., That's for boys, not girls), and gender equality (e.g., Anyone can do it). Furthermore, nouns referring to people typically expressed gender, even though speakers had a choice of whether or not to mention gender (e.g., they could have said "person" or "child" rather than "girl"). When referring to pictures of people in the picture book, explicit reference to gender (by use of gendered nouns such as "girl" or gendered pronouns such as "she") exceeded 90%. Among all these devices, gendered nouns and generics were by far the most common. Both mothers and children frequently used generics to make sweeping category-wide statements. Even among 2-year-olds, who used generics far less frequently than the other two age groups, 7 out of 24 children and 21 out of 24 mothers used at least one generic. (At ages 4 and 6, the numbers were 45 out of 48 children and all of the mothers.) For children, and for conversations with boys, such statements were especially likely to focus on gendered categories (e.g., boys, girls, men, women), as contrasted to non-gendered categories (e.g., ballet dancers, kids, grown-ups).

What changes were taking place with age? First, as noted above, 2-year-olds do not show the preference for affirming stereotypes that we see among 4- and 6-year-olds. Second, there were striking age increases in the frequency of generics, gender contrasts, and gender equality statements. Interestingly, these increases were found both among children and among mothers. It is therefore difficult to localize the source of these changes—are they due to increases between 2 and 4 years of age in children's attention to gender, or due to changes in the complexity and sophistication of parents' speech to children, or both?

Regarding sex-of-child effects: For the most part, patterns are quite similar in conversations with boys vs. girls. However, three differences did emerge. First, overall, conversations with boys focused more on males, and conversations with girls focused more on females. This is not too surprising, given that these conversations included references to the child himself or herself, thereby of necessity biasing talk toward same-sex references. More interesting, when using generic noun phrases, conversations with girls were markedly more likely than conversations with boys to include non-gendered generics. They focused on dimensions *other than* gender—primarily age ("old people," "grown-ups," "little kids," "babies," "teenagers," "big kids"), occupation ("somebody that cuts wood," "a sailor"), or people in general ("you" [meaning "one"]; "either" [males or females]), but also occasionally ethnicity ("African Americans," "Indians") or other properties ("you have to be responsible," "if you're handicapped," "a babysitter"). Framed slightly differently, generics to and from boys were more likely to focus on the dimension of gender, whereas generics to and from girls were more open to other means of classifying people. Finally, boys were more likely than girls to produce *negative-valence* utterances about gender-stereotypical activities, focusing on what people cannot do, should not do, don't like to do, etc. This would be consistent with the notion that boys are more concerned with establishing boundaries for what is appropriate with regard to gender (Leaper, 1994).

Focusing on sex-of-referent effects—whether the talk concerned males or females—there was an unexpected inconsistency in the direction of effects. When expressing attitudes toward stereotypes, there was a *female* bias, indicating that speakers affirmed gender stereotypes more frequently when talking about females than when talking about males. In contrast, for both generics and gender-ostensive labeling, there was a *male* bias, indicating that speakers produced more generics about males than females, and labeled males more than females. In other words, females received more emphasis in speakers' explicit gender stereotyping statements, whereas males received more emphasis in speakers' implicit talk about gender and gender categories. The implicit and explicit measures therefore present contrasting portraits of whether males or females are more gender-typed in maternal speech. We had expected a male bias overall, given past research indicating that people are more stereotyped in their notions of maleness (Hort, Fagot, & Leinbach, 1990). The puzzle is why there was a female bias in gender-stereotype attitudes. We return to this issue in the General Discussion.

Finally, we found a variety of strong differences in how speakers talked about pages that depicted gender-consistent activities (e.g., girl playing with doll) vs. pages that depicted gender-inconsistent activities (e.g., boy playing with doll). Gender-inconsistent pages were associated with several different kinds of talk: more counter-stereotypical attitudes, more generics (for mothers only), more gender-ostensive labeling, more gender contrasts, and more gender equality statements. These reflect *both* greater focus on gender categories *and* more gender-egalitarianism. The counter-stereotypical attitudes and gender equality statements suggest that on gender-inconsistent pages, speakers provide *less* stereotyping; in contrast, the greater use of generics, gender-ostensive labeling, and gender contrasts suggest that on gender-inconsistent pages, speakers provide *more* attention to the dimension of gender. It seems that both effects are going on simultaneously. In terms of *explicit* messages, speakers more frequently mention *counter-stereotyped* behaviors on gender-inconsistent pages. However, in terms of *implicit* messages, speakers display a greater focus on gender categories on gender-inconsistent pages. This cluster of results confirms that implicit and explicit messages can sometimes be in conflict with one another.

In summary, the analyses we have presented reveal a rich array of messages regarding gender, in the language of mothers and their young children. These findings support and complement past research indicating that parents convey gender stereotypes to young children, by rewarding gender-consistent behaviors or discouraging cross-gender toy play (e.g., Eisenberg et al., 1985; Fagot, 1978; Fagot et al., 1985; Lytton & Romney, 1991). What may perhaps be surprising in these data is that parent and child language is consistently sensitive to the dimensions under study: age, sex-of-child, sex-of-referent, and page consistency all are associated with subtle variations in speech. Another consistent theme to emerge from this chapter is the contrast between explicit and implicit messages. In their overt, explicit messages, mothers in this sample are primarily gender-egalitarian in their input. However, what mothers imply indirectly conveys additional, gender-typed messages. In the General Discussion we turn to the question of what effects (if any) these varied messages might have on children's developing gender concepts. Meanwhile, Chapter IV focuses on the most frequent and implicit means of focusing on gender, namely, reference to gender *categories* by means of generic noun phrases (e.g., "Are *boys* allowed to be ballet dancers?").

NOTES

6. All eta-squared (η^2) results that we report use the partial η^2 formula ($SS_{effect}/(SS_{effect}+SS_{error})$). Tabachnick and Fidell (1989) suggest that partial η^2 is an appropriate alternate computation of η^2.

7. The term "ostension" comes from "ostensive definition" in philosophy, which means that one labels an object by pointing to it while naming (Quine, 1960). Here, our purpose in using this phrase is to emphasize that the function of these utterances is to provide a gender label and thereby classify the instance as a member of a gender category. The label does not mention gender only incidentally.

8. We use the phrase "activity sex" as short-hand for the more cumbersome phrase "sex (male or female) that is stereotypically associated with the target activity." We do not mean to imply that certain activities are inherently male or female.

IV. TALK ABOUT CATEGORIES VERSUS INDIVIDUALS (GENERICS VS. NON-GENERICS)

One of the major research questions that this research was designed to explore concerns how generic references to gender differ from non-generic references to gender. Recall that generic noun phrases are those that refer to a category as a whole (e.g., "girls," "men," "sailors"), and can be distinguished from noun phrases that refer to individuals (e.g., "Sally," "those men," "the sailor"). Generics are distinctive in referring to properties that are relatively enduring, non-accidental, and divorced from specific context (Carlson & Pelletier, 1995; Gelman, 2003; Lyons, 1977; Prasada, 2000). Therefore, generics concerning gender express particularly powerful and generalizable properties.

The analyses in Chapter III reveal that generics were a particularly frequent form of reference to gender-based categories. Aside from expressing direct attitudes about gender stereotypes, generics were the most common means of referring to gender. Furthermore, they showed a number of intriguing patterns: systematic increase between 2 and 4 years of age, bias toward reference to males, different profiles for conversations with girls vs. boys (with more gendered generics for boys than girls). A comparison of generics to non-generics is important for determining how distinctive generics are. That is, are these patterns special to generics, or somehow a reflection of the talk more generally? An answer to this question will also help us determine what information children hear and provide regarding gender categories. We explored this question in three ways: examining differences in the <u>content</u> that was expressed, examining differences in utterance <u>form</u>, and examining differences in utterance <u>modality</u>. All analyses reported in this chapter compared person-references that were generic or non-generic (thereby excluding utterances that did not include explicit reference to a person by means of a noun or pronoun). As in Chapter III, all post-hoc tests were conducted using the Bonferroni correction.

CONTENT DIFFERENCES

There are two primary aspects of utterance content that are of interest: the sex of the referent being addressed and the attitude expressed toward the gender-stereotyped activity depicted on the page. Do generics differ from non-generics, in either respect? We examined each aspect in a separate analysis, below.

Sex of Referent

We conducted a 3 (age group: 2, 4, 6) × 2 (speaker: mother, child) × 2 (child sex: boy, girl) × 2 (generic: generic, non-generic) × 2 (page type: consistent, inconsistent) × 3 (sex-of-referent: male, female, non-gendered) ANOVA. The dependent measure was the number of utterances of a given type per speaker, divided by the total number of on-task utterances for that speaker. Here we report only those effects involving generic–non-generic differences.

We obtained a main effect of generics, $F(1, 132) = 135.45$, $p < .001$, $\eta^2 = .51$, indicating that speakers produced more non-generics than generics. We also obtained a generic × speaker interaction, $F(1,132) = 6.93$, $p < .01$, $\eta^2 = .05$, indicating that children produced as many generics as mothers ($M = 12.17$ and 12.31, $SD = 15.98$ and 11.69, for children and mothers, respectively), even though mothers produced many more non-generics than children ($M = 29.21$ and 39.31, $SD = 18.59$ and 12.67, for children and mothers, respectively, $p < .001$). In other words, generics represented a higher proportion of *children's* person references to the target activity, than of *mothers'* person references to the target activity. Thus, children are relatively more likely than their mothers to phrase information in terms of categorywide generalizations.

There was also a generic × sex-of-referent interaction, $F(2,264) = 54.41$, $p < .001$, $\eta^2 = .29$, indicating that generics are relatively more likely than non-generics to be ungendered (nearly one-third of generic utterances, compared to only about one-sixth of non-generic utterances). For non-generics, ungendered utterances were less frequent than either male or female utterances, $p < .001$. In contrast, for generics, ungendered utterances were as frequent as both male and female utterances, n.s. This interaction was tempered somewhat by age, in a generic × sex-of-referent × age interaction, $F(4, 264) = 4.14$, $p < .005$, $\eta^2 = .06$. This 3-way interaction indicates that for non-generics, conversations with older children were less likely to contain gendered referents than conversations with younger children. In contrast, for generics, conversations with the 6-year-olds were relatively more likely to contain gendered referents than conversations with younger children. Finally, there was a generic × sex-of-reference × child

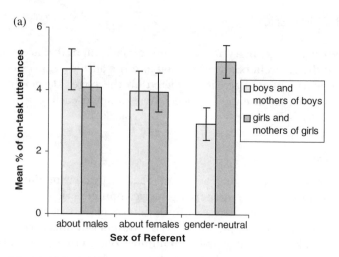

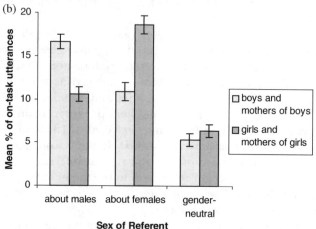

Note: Vertical bars depict standard errors of the means. (a) Generics: (b) Non-generics.

FIGURE 15.—Mean percentage of on-task utterances as a function of scope (generic vs. nongeneric), sex-of-referent, and child sex.

sex interaction, $F(2, 264) = 28.20$, $p < .001$, $\eta^2 = .18$. This interaction is shown in Figure 15. Whereas generics showed a slight male-bias, $p = .062$, non-generics showed a sex-of-child bias (e.g., more non-generics regarding females than males in conversations with girls, $p < .001$, and more non-generics regarding males than females in conversations with boys, $p < .001$).

Attitude Toward Gender-Stereotypical Content

We conducted a 3 (age group: 2, 4, 6) × 2 (speaker: mother, child) × 2 (child sex: boy, girl) × 2 (generic: generic, non-generic) × 2 (page type:

consistent, inconsistent) × 3 (attitude: affirm, deny, or neutral) ANOVA. The dependent measure was the number of utterances of a given type per speaker, divided by the total number of on-task utterances for that speaker. Here we report only those effects involving generic-non-generic differences.

As in the analysis of sex-of-referent, we obtained a main effect of generics, $F(1, 132) = 151.49$, $p < .001$, $\eta^2 = .53$, and a generic × speaker interaction, $F(1, 132) = 9.92$, $p < .005$, $\eta^2 = .07$. There was also a generic × age group interaction, $F(2, 132) = 3.20$, $p < .05$, $\eta^2 = .05$, indicating that generics increased markedly in frequency with age (more generics in conversations with 6-year-olds than 4- or 2-year-olds, $p < .05$, and more generics in conversations with 4-year-olds than 2-year-olds, $p < .005$), whereas non-generics stayed fairly constant over the period of 2–4 to 6 years of age (no significant pairwise differences).

The remaining effects all involved attitude. There was a generic × attitude × speaker interaction, $F(2, 264) = 55.69$, $p < .001$, $\eta^2 = .30$. This indicates that, for both generics and non-generics, children affirm gender stereotypes more than they deny them, $p < .001$, and rarely express a neutral attitude (neutral less than affirming or denying, $p < .01$). In contrast, for both generics and non-generics, mothers affirm and deny stereotypes equally, but most often express a neutral attitude (neutral greater than affirming or denying, $p < .001$). The effect of generics indicates that the attitude × speaker interaction is more sizeable for non-generics, simply because non-generics are more frequent.

There was also a generic × attitude × consistency interaction, $F(2, 264) = 48.24$, $p < .001$, $\eta^2 = .27$. This indicates that, for both generics and non-generics, speakers affirm gender stereotypes more on consistent than inconsistent pages ($p < .01$), and they deny generic stereotypes more on inconsistent than consistent pages ($p < .01$). See Figure 16. However, this effect is stronger for non-generics than generics. Furthermore, generics and non-generics diverge for neutral attitudes. For non-generics, speakers express neutral attitudes equally often on consistent and inconsistent pages, whereas for generics, speakers express neutral attitudes more on inconsistent pages, $p < .05$.

Finally, there were two four-way interactions: generic × attitude × consistency × age, $F(4, 264) = 3.77$, $p = .005$, $\eta^2 = .05$, and generic × attitude × consistency × child sex, $F(2, 264) = 3.91$, $p < .05$, $\eta^2 = .03$. The four-way interaction involving age reveals that, for both generics and non-generics, page consistency predicted attitudes toward gender stereotypes: relatively more affirmations on gender-consistent pages and relatively more denials on gender-inconsistent pages. In other words, for both generics and non-generics, presence of stereotype-inconsistent pages was associated with relatively fewer stereotype-affirming utterances. However, the size of this effect was greater for non-generics than for generics, par-

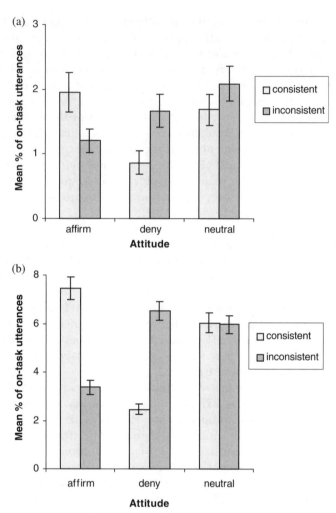

Note: Vertical bars depict standard errors of the means. (a) Generics: (b) Non-generics.

FIGURE 16.—Mean percentage of on-task utterances as a function of scope (generic vs. non-generic), attitude, and page consistency.

ticularly for speech to and from the youngest children. Specifically, the only times when consistency did *not* yield a significant effect was with generics (stereotype affirmations and denials at age 2, and stereotype denials at age 6).

The four-way interaction involving child sex shows that the attitude × consistency interaction described above was greater for non-generics than for generics, particularly for speech to and from girls. Specifically, the only times when consistency did not yield a significant effect was with generic speech to and from girls (no significant effect for either stereotype affirmations or stereotype denials).

FORM DIFFERENCES

References to people vary considerably in form, some of which mark gender and others of which do not. The English language has many devices for conveying the gender of a noun phrase, including labels for gender categories (e.g., boy, girl, man, woman, lady, fireman, ballerina), gendered pronouns (e.g., he, she, him, her), and gendered proper names (e.g., Jason, Jennifer). Other means of referring to people are ungendered, including labels for non-gender categories (e.g., firefighter, cheerleader, grown-up), non-gendered pronouns (e.g., it, they, me, you), and non-gendered proper names (e.g., Pat, Alex). This next analysis examined whether generics and non-generics differ in the extent to which they mark gender explicitly.

For each reference to a person or persons, we tallied how many were male gendered in form, how many were female gendered in form, and how many were neutral gendered in form, and divided by the total number of on-task utterances for that speaker. Note that gender of the form is partly independent of gender of the referent itself. For example, a speaker may say, "They can?", referring to boys (as made clear by prior context), which would be gender neutral in form although male in content. We conducted a 3 (age: 2, 4, 6 years) × 2 (child sex: boy, girl) × 2 (speaker: child, mother) × 2 (generic: generic, non-generic) × 3 (form of utterance sex: male, female, other) ANOVA.

We report only those effects involving form-of-utterance, as these are the focus of this section. There was a main effect of form, $F(2, 264) = 99.69$, $p < .001$, $\eta^2 = .43$, indicating that non-gendered utterances were most frequent, and that male utterances were more frequent than female utterances. There was a form × age interaction, $F(4, 264) = 3.43$, $p < .01$, $\eta^2 = .05$, indicating that the male advantage increased with child age. Specifically, there was no male advantage in conversations with 2-year-olds, but there was at ages 4 and 6 ($p < .05$). There was a form × speaker interaction, $F(2, 264) = 15.87$, $p < .001$, $\eta^2 = .11$, indicating that children were relatively more likely than mothers to produce female-gendered utterances, $p < .05$, whereas mothers were more likely than children to produce gender-neutral utterances, $p < .001$.

Finally, there were two effects involving generics (see Figure 17). There was a generic × form interaction, $F(2, 264) = 81.20$, $p < .001$, $\eta^2 = .38$, indicating that generics were relatively more likely than non-generics to

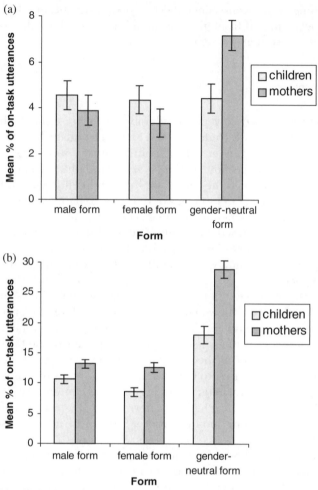

Note: Vertical bars depict standard errors of the means. (a) Generics: (b) Non-generics.

FIGURE 17.—Mean percentage of on-task utterances as a function of scope (generic vs. non-generic), form, and speaker.

be gendered (either male or female) as opposed to gender neutral. This effect was tempered by speaker, in a generic × form × speaker interaction, $F(2, 264) = 3.41, p < .05, \eta^2 = .025$. This three-way interaction indicates that this effect is particularly striking for children. Gender neutral form is more common than either male or female form, all $p < .001$, *except* in the case of children's generics, for which male and female forms are as frequent as gender neutral forms.

70

MODALITY DIFFERENCES

Although the picture books specifically asked about "can" (e.g., "Who can chop wood?"), speakers did not restrict themselves to discussion of permission or ability (both of which are implied by the word "can"). They also discussed existence (e.g., "This is a firewoman," "[Girl's name] takes ballet"), preference (e.g., "That's right, boys like to play with dolls all the time"), and obligation (e.g., "Do you think that boys should maybe help with that project?"). For ease of expression, we refer to these various modalities as Can, Do, Like, and Should. The analyses in this section examined whether generics and non-generics differ in the kinds of modalities they express.

For each reference to the target activity, we tallied how many expressed each of the four modalities: Can, Do, Like, and Should, and divided by the total number of on-task utterances for that speaker. We conducted a 3 (age: 2, 4, 6 years) × 2 (child sex: boy, girl) × 2 (speaker: child, mother) × 2 (generic: generic, non-generic) × 4 (modality: Can, Do, Like, Should) ANOVA.

We report only those effects involving modality, as these are the focus of this section. There was a main effect of modality, $F(3, 396) = 267.74$, $p < .001$, $\eta^2 = .67$, indicating a consistent ordering of the four types of modality: Can > Do > Like > Should. That is, utterances referring to permission or ability (Can) were most frequent, followed by reference to existence (Do), followed by preference (Like), followed by obligation (Should), all $p < .005$. However, modality interacted with several other factors. Modality interacted with age group, $F(6, 396) = 18.53$, $p < .001$, $\eta^2 = .22$, such that in conversations with 2-year-olds, Can and Do were not significantly different in frequency, in contrast to conversations with 4- and 6-year-olds, where Can was most frequent, $p < .001$. Modality also interacted with sex of child, $F(3, 396) = 4.71$, $p < .005$, $\eta^2 = .03$, such that conversations with girls involved more reference to Can than conversations with boys, $p < .05$. Modality interacted with speaker, $F(3, 396) = 46.82$, $p < .001$, $\eta^2 = .26$, indicating that children produced Can more often than mothers, $p < .005$, whereas mothers produced Do, Like, and Should more often than children, $p < .005$.

Finally, the remaining effects involved generics. Most importantly, we obtained a generic × modality interaction, $F(3, 396) = 46.69$, $p < .001$, $\eta^2 = .26$, and a generic × modality × speaker interaction, $F(3, 396) = 10.16$, $p < .001$, $\eta^2 = .07$. (See Figure 18.) For both mothers and children, generics were relatively more focused on "can," whereas non-generics were relatively more focused on "do." Also, the ordering by modality differs for generics vs. non-generics. For *mothers*, generics were ordered as follows: Can, Do > Should > Like, whereas non-generics were ordered as follows: Do > Can > Like > Should. (All effects significant at $p < .005$.) Thus, for mothers, generic utterances were relatively more focused than non-generic

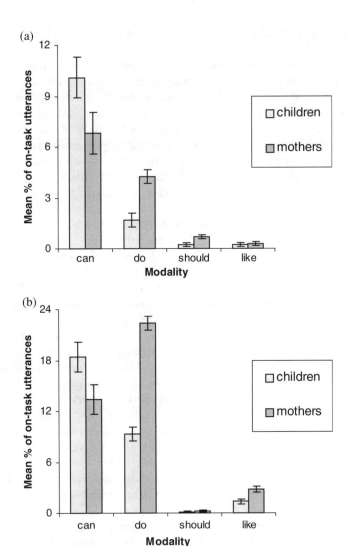

Note: Vertical bars depict standard errors of the means. (a) Generics: (b) Non-generics.

FIGURE 18.—Mean percentage of on-task utterances as a function of scope (generic vs. non-generic), modality, and speaker.

utterances on what people *can* and *should* do, whereas non-generic utterances were relatively more focused than generic utterances on what people *do* and *like to* do.

For *children*, generics were ordered as follows: Can > Do > Should > Like, whereas non-generics were ordered as follows: Can > Do > Like > Should. (All effects significant at $p < .005$). Although subtle, this difference indicates again that generics focus relatively more on what people *should* do, whereas non-generics focus relatively more on what people *like to* do. Overall, for both mothers and children, generics seem therefore more focused on hypothetical possibility, whereas non-generics seem more focused on actuality.

We also obtained a generic × modality × age group interaction, $F(6, 396) = 2.34, p < .05, \eta^2 = .03$. This interaction largely reflects the small number of generics in conversations with 2-year-olds. As a result, conversations with 2-year-olds are the only place where we don't find sizeable modality effects (i.e., the only significant modality effect involved more Do than Like generics, $p < .05$). In part this finding may reflect the relative paucity of modal auxiliaries (such as *can*, *could*, or *should*) in this age group (see Shatz & Wilcox, 1991, for a review).

SUMMARY AND DISCUSSION

Both mothers and children frequently referred to gender *categories* in contrast to gendered *individuals*, as when a 6-year-old boy said, "*Girls* aren't that much into sports" (meaning "*Girls generally* aren't that much into sports") or when a 4-year-old girl said, "*A mommy*" [can feed a baby] (meaning "*Any mommy* [can feed a baby]"). We refer to these as generic noun phrases. By definition, generic noun phrases are broader in scope than non-generic noun phrases (e.g., "That is *a lady* sewing a dress, right?"), and children are sensitive to this scope difference (Hollander et al., 2002). The question that motivated the analyses presented in this chapter is whether generic expressions differ in other respects from non-generics. Are general references to gender distinctive in the contents they express, their contexts of use, or the attitudes they convey?

The portrait that emerges from the range of analyses we conducted is that both children and mothers talk differently when making generic references to gender as distinct from specific reference to gendered individuals. Children as well as mothers differentiate generics from non-generics both in the meanings that are expressed and in their formal expression. With regard to content, generics display a slight male bias, in contrast to non-generics, which display a sex-of-child bias. This indicates that, although each parent–child dyad focuses more on the gender of the child who is present, males are more likely to be the focus of category-wide generalizations. Generics are also more likely to be ungendered in content than non-generics. This latter result reflects a basic conceptual distinction between individuals and categories: Individuals are nearly always gendered, and their gender is typically accessible, even to coders who don't know the participants in the conversation. In contrast, generic categories are not always gendered; one can choose to focus on either a gendered generic category (e.g., "boys") or an ungendered generic category (e.g., "little kids").

Interestingly, there is a seemingly paradoxical shift in form (vs. content), when comparing generics vs. non-generics. In form, generics are more likely to be gendered than non-generics (e.g., "So boys and girls can learn to sew" [generic, gendered in form] vs. "A girl's playing football" [non-generic, gendered in form]). This contrasts with the finding that in *content*, generics are *less* likely to be gendered than non-generics (e.g., "Grown-ups can be firefighters?" [generic, non-gendered in content] vs. "Do you know anybody who's a firefighter?" [non-generic, non-gendered in content]). Although at first this contrast between form and content may appear contradictory, it is a direct consequence of the fact that generics are abstract (and hence divorced from immediate context), whereas non-generics refer to particular individuals, often in a known context. Thus, when referring to individuals, gender content can often be inferred from context, even when the form is agnostic. Words such as "I," "you," and "this person" don't express gender in their form, but the gender of their referents is obvious. In contrast, when referring to categories, gender content can be inferred only if it is stated explicitly, either in the noun phrase itself (e.g., "boys") or in an antecedent utterance (e.g., "boys" antecedent to the pronoun "they"). This contradiction can be illustrated with the word "neighbor." If someone says, "Here's a picture of my neighbor" (non-generic), chances are you would be able to figure out the gender of the neighbor, based on the picture. But if someone says, "Good fences make good neighbors" (with apologies to Robert Frost), then no gender content is implied.

In this study, speakers made use of many devices to refer to gendered individuals in non-gendered ways, especially non-gendered pronouns (I, you, they, this person). For generics, only the word "they" can be used to refer to a gendered category in a non-gendered manner. In other words, there is a tighter link between gender content and gender form for generics than for non-generics.

For attitudes, we find that both generics and non-generics vary as a function of page consistency. As noted earlier, this finding is important, because it suggests that the effects of page consistency are far-reaching, and not limited to mention of pictures in the book. In other words, even when discussing broad categories, speakers express less-stereotyped attitudes on stereotype-inconsistent pages than on stereotype-consistent pages. At the same time, however, the effects of consistency are more marked for non-generics than for generics. This interaction suggests that generics are not as easily swayed by context as non-generics. This finding is consistent with the idea that generics deal with abstractions (e.g., boys as a generalized category) that transcend the particulars of a given context.

74

The findings for modality are intriguing for what they reveal about the semantics of generics. Generics are more likely than non-generics to focus on what a person or persons *can* do, and on what a person or persons *should* do. Both "can" and "should" deal with proscriptions—in contrast to descriptions (actualities). This is consistent with the idea that generic categories are not simply compilations of observed regularities, but rather reflect an idealized set of expectations, rules, and norms. Generics thus seem to be used to express societal expectations about gender.

Altogether, the numerous differences between generics and non-generics suggest that generic categories of gender are a distinct sort of concept from gendered individuals, for both children and their mothers. The patterns of speech are distributed differently, and reveal that in maternal speech, gender generics convey a distinct cluster of implications.

V. BEYOND THE INDIVIDUAL: DISCOURSE PATTERNS AND CORRELATIONAL ANALYSES

This chapter goes beyond analyses of individual utterances to examine the *patterns* of mother–child interaction in discourse context, as well as correlational analyses involving maternal talk, child talk, and measures of gender-typing and gender constancy. We focus on four questions. First, how do mothers respond to child stereotyping? When a child expresses a gender stereotype, does the mother affirm, negate, or question the child? Second, who leads the way in introducing generics—children or mothers? We have found remarkable parallels between mothers and children in the use of generics over time: generics steadily increase from 2 to 4–6 years of age, for both mothers and children. Are children simply following mothers' lead, in generic expression? At what age, if any, do children introduce generic talk into the conversation? Third, how closely do mothers and children match one another in the kinds of talk they provide? This question will be examined by conducting correlations between maternal speech and child speech. Fourth, how closely does talk during the book session correspond to assessments of gender-typing and gender constancy? Follow-up *t*-tests were conducted using the Bonferroni correction.

MOTHERS' RESPONSES TO CHILD STEREOTYPING

The question we address in this section is how mothers responded to children's gender-stereotyped statements. Did mothers support, contradict, or question such statements? To examine this issue, we first identified all utterances in which a child affirmed a gender stereotype. As described in the Transcriptions and Coding (Chapter II), gender-stereotypical remarks were identified on the basis of utterance content and valence, along with information about the set-up of the page (i.e., sex of target and consistency). Stereotype affirmations could be generic or individual in scope, and they could entail either endorsing a gender stereotype or rejecting a counter-

TABLE 12

MEAN NUMBER OF CHILD STEREOTYPE AFFIRMATIONS AS A FUNCTION OF CHILD AGE AND SEX,
USED IN DISCOURSE ANALYSIS OF MATERNAL RESPONSES

	Child Sex	
	Male	Female
2 years	23.25 (21.99)	24.75 (19.12)
4 years	32.83 (12.50)	27.83 (14.39)
6 years	30.08 (14.23)	33.25 (18.99)

Note.—SDs are in parentheses.

stereotypical possibility. They could also involve either explicit mention of the person(s), or implicit mention of the person(s). For example, all of the following child utterances were coded as stereotype affirmations: "My dad can" [chop wood]; "Because ballet dancers are girls!"; "I'm not, I can't be a seamstress" [said by a boy]; "Little girls don't" [take out the trash]; "Of course" [in response to "Do you think Grandpa could catch a frog?"]; "I don't want to" [in response to a boy being asked, "Who can be a cheer-leader?"]. Altogether, there were 2,064 such statements. Table 12 lists the mean number of children's stereotype affirmations as a function of child sex and age.

The maternal utterance immediately following each such statement by the child was then coded into one or more of four basic categories: affirm, negate, question, and other.[9] Questions were further subdivided into question-repeat (mother repeats the child's statement in question form, or affirms what the child says in question form), question-expand (mother provides a question that introduces a new person(s) relating to the target activity), and question-why (mother asks why). (Questions that did not fit into one of those three categories were coded as "other.") Finally, question-expands were further subdivided into those that mentioned the *same* gender category as the child had stated ("Can little girls do sewing?" in response to child saying that "big women" can do sewing), those that mentioned a *new* gender category from what the child had stated ("Can daddies knit?" in response to child saying that moms can knit a sweater), and those that were *neutral* or unspecified with respect to gender ("Do you think anybody else could?" in response to child saying that "Billy" [pseudonym] can take out the trash).

What implications do these different coding categories have? Obviously, affirmations are most supportive of the stereotype and negations are most overtly critical of the stereotype. In addition, one might consider questions to be implicitly critical of the stereotype, to greater or lesser degree. Questions that expand to a new gender category are the most openly suggestive to children that they consider a counter-stereotypical example, in contrast to either questions that expand to the same gender category, or questions that expand to an unspecified gender category. Finally, question-repeats are more ambiguous, and for some mothers simply a device to keep the conversation going without committing to either affirmation or negation, for other mothers a challenge, as if to ask, "Are you sure about that?" With these possible interpretations in mind, we now turn to the analyses.

One primary goal was to analyze the relative frequency of these different codes as a function of different child factors and utterance types. In order to do so, we first needed to transform the scores so that they were all on the same scale and the data from each participant was weighted equally. Therefore, all numbers are presented as percentages of total number of maternal responses for each dyad. For example, if a child provided 10 stereotyping statements, and the mother affirmed 3 of them, then the dyad was given a score of 30% affirmations.

Overall Patterns

The first question concerns the overall patterns of response. How did mothers in this task generally respond to stereotyping statements by their children? As can be seen in Table 13, three categories of response were by far the most frequent: affirm (33%), other (29%), and question-repeat (20%). Thus, when children provided a stereotype-consistent statement, mothers' most frequent response was to affirm what the child said. Explicitly negating the child's stereotype was extremely rare (less than 2%). However, the relative frequency of question-repeats is interesting, in that they may be intended as an implicit means of challenging the child's statement, by questioning rather than affirming what the child said. It is also notable that when

TABLE 13

MEAN PERCENTAGE OF MOTHERS' RESPONSES TO CHILDREN'S STEREOTYPE AFFIRMATIONS, AS A FUNCTION OF CODING CATEGORY AND CHILD SEX

Coding Category	Boys	Girls
Affirm	29.22 (17.42)	36.78 (23.03)
Question-repeat	23.58 (16.56)	16.43 (14.20)
Question-expand (new gender)	5.98 (6.18)	5.19 (7.04)
Question-expand (gender-neutral)	5.00 (4.68)	5.49 (6.86)
Question-expand (same-gender)	2.74 (3.48)	2.53 (3.02)
Question-why	3.22 (4.96)	1.69 (3.28)
Negate	2.31 (3.50)	1.21 (3.57)
Other	27.96 (14.25)	30.68 (18.11)

Note.—SDs are in parentheses.

78

mothers provided a new example in question form (e.g., "Can women chop wood?"), the person or persons was more likely to be contrasting in gender to the example the child provided (question-expand (new-gender)) than to be of the same gender as the example the child provided (question-expand (same-gender)), 5.6% vs. 2.6% of responses, a significant difference by paired-t (71) = 3.51, p = .001.

Child Age and Child Sex

We then examined the effects of two between-subjects factors: child age and child sex. Analyses of child age indicated that mothers more often asked older children than younger children to explain their stereotyping statements. Specifically, mothers provided "why" questions significantly less often to 2-year-olds (0.5% of responses) than to either 4-year-olds (4% of responses) or 6-year-olds (3% of responses), both $ps < .01$. There was also an unexpected finding indicating that mothers of 6-year-olds were more likely than mothers of 4-year-olds to provide an expansion question concerning the same-gender as the child had mentioned, $p < .02$. Otherwise, however, the patterns were quite stable over age.

Patterns for boys vs. girls showed a consistent tendency for mothers to be more challenging of boys' stereotyping than of girls': fewer agreements (29.2% boys, 36.8% girls), more negations (2.3% boys, 1.2% girls), more questioning repeats (23.6% boys, 16.4% girls), and more "why" questions (3.2% boys, 1.7% girls). Of all these comparisons, however, only one was statistically significant considered individually, namely, that mothers of boys were more likely than mothers of girls to repeat the child's statement in a questioning tone (question-repeat), $t(70) = 1.97$, $p = .053$. However, when we created a composite score of all the negative or challenging responses (negations, questioning-repeats, and "why"-questions), we found a clear sex-of-child difference, with mothers posing more challenging responses to boys compared to girls, $t(70) = 2.55$, $p < .02$.

Valence, Scope, Page Consistency, and Sex of Referent

The remaining analyses involved four within-subjects factors: valence of utterance (positive or negative), scope of utterance (generic or individual), consistency of activity in book (stereotype-consistent or stereotype-inconsistent), and sex of referent (male or female). Because of the relatively small numbers of cases, particularly when the data are broken down by the within-subjects factors, we conducted each of these analyses independently.

For each analysis, we first calculated a Yule's Q score for each dyad,[10] then conducted a t-test comparing these scores to chance (0), for each of the coding categories considered separately: affirm, negate, question-repeat, question-expand (same-gender), question-expand (new-gender), question-expand (gender-neutral), question-why, and other. Separate *t*-tests were used because of the lack of independence of the different coding categories, making a multivariate analysis inappropriate. To minimize Type I error, we only report results that are significant at $p < .01$ or smaller. Although all children did produce at least some stereotyping statements, some children did not provide stereotyping statements for both values of a factor (e.g., some children produced no generic stereotyping statements; others provided no negative-valence stereotyping statements; one child produced no stereotyping statements about females). For each analysis, we excluded those cases in which data were missing from one or the other level of that particular factor.

Valence

For this analysis, we examined responses to child utterances that involved a positive valence (e.g., "I know girls play with dolls") and compared them to responses to child utterances that involved a negative valence (e.g., "Boys aren't really fond of playing dolls though"). Twenty-three children provided no negative-valence stereotypical statements, leaving an *N* of 49. Here several differences emerged. Mothers were much more likely to affirm positive-valence than negative-valence statements, $M = 37\%$ vs. 7%, Yule's $Q = .76$, $t(48) = 14.55$, $p < .001$. Positive-valence statements were more likely than negative-valence statements to be followed by questions that suggested extension to others—either neutral in gender, $Ms = 6\%$ vs. 4.6%, Yule's $Q = .51$, $t(48) = 5.23$, $p < .001$, or of a new gender, $M = 6\%$ vs. 4%, Yule's $Q = .54$, $t(48) = 6.42$, $p < .001$. Finally, negative-valence statements were followed by more why-questions than positive-valence statements, 13% vs. 1%, Yule's $Q = -.42$, $t(48) = -5.25$, $p < .001$. Altogether, it is clear that mothers responded quite differently to positive- vs. negative-valence statements on the part of children. Whereas mothers are likely to accept positive-valence statements of stereotyping, and to ask questions that simply extended such statements to others, they appear to be more critical and probing in response to negative-valence stereotypical statements. Children's negative-valence statements were followed by fewer positive responses from mothers, as well as more questions challenging the child's statement, and more why-questions probing children's reasoning.

Scope

Here we compared maternal responses to generic vs. non-generic stereotypical statements. Twenty-three children provided no generic stereotypical statements, leaving an N of 49. Two differences were significant. Mothers provided relatively fewer affirmations for generics than non-generics, $M = 23\%$ vs. 34%, respectively, Yule's $Q = -.38$, $t(48) = -3.70$, $p < .001$. Mothers were also relatively less likely to provide questions that expanded in a gender-neutral way (e.g., "What about some other people that can play with trucks?") in response to generics than non-generics, $M = 3\%$ vs. 6%, respectively, Yule's $Q = -.39$, $t(48) = -3.77$, $p < .001$. Altogether, these differences suggest that mothers more actively directed their children toward anti-stereotyped possibilities, when responding to generic statements vs. individual statements.

Page consistency

This analysis compared maternal responses when the book page displayed a gender-consistent activity (e.g., a man chopping wood) vs. when the book page displayed a gender-inconsistent activity (e.g., a woman chopping wood). Five children provided statements about either only consistent or only inconsistent pages, leaving an N of 67. Mothers provided more affirmations when the page was gender-consistent than when it was gender-inconsistent, 35% vs. 29%, respectively, Yule's $Q = .19$, $t(66) = 2.68$, $p < .01$. Perhaps the presence of the gender-inconsistent page suggested other, less stereotyping possibilities to mothers.

Sex of referent

This analysis compared maternal responses to stereotypical statements regarding males and maternal responses to stereotypical statements regarding females. One child provided no stereotypical statements about females, leaving an N of 71. No significant differences emerged in these analyses.

Summary

Mothers' responses to children's stereotyping statements are unexpectedly revealing. Despite the fact that these mothers do not generally produce gender-stereotypical statements in their own speech overall, they rarely negate their children's gender-stereotyping statements. The single most common response to children's stereotyping statements was to affirm what the child said. When mothers did express skepticism, it was typically mild, either repeating the child's statement in a questioning tone (e.g., "Um, well, you, you think girls look better in ballet?"), or suggesting an extension to the other gender (e.g., "And have you ever played hopscotch?" [said to a boy]). These patterns were quite stable over ages and child genders.

Beyond these overall patterns, the most striking findings concerned valence, how mothers responded to positive- vs. negative-valence statements on the part of children. Positive-valence stereotypes (e.g., "Sometimes boys" [can be a firefighter]) were treated as fairly benign: affirmed one-third of the time, very rarely negated, rarely receiving a request for explanation. In contrast, negative-valence stereotypes (e.g., "Boys can't be cheerleaders") were responded to the most negatively: negated as often as affirmed, and more often followed by requests for explanation. These differences suggest an interesting bias in maternal construals of child stereotyping: positive affirmations of stereotypes are not considered problematic or demanding of explanation. In contrast, negative affirmations of stereotypes lead to more debate and concern. These patterns may provide some insight into the perpetuation of gender stereotypes, despite mothers' fairly gender-egalitarian attitudes. For mothers, "positive" stereotyping is unremarkable and unproblematic, and only "negative" stereotyping demands attention and response—yet for children, it may be that both positive and negative stereotyping contribute to gender-stereotyped beliefs.

Finally, with regard to scope, we saw that mothers were less likely to affirm generic stereotypes than non-generic stereotypes. Mothers were also less likely to extend the child's response with an open-ended question. It seems that mothers considered generic stereotypes to be more serious than non-generic stereotypes. This finding is consistent with the earlier generic/non-generic differences, suggesting a systematic difference in how generics vs. non-generics are interpreted.

INTRODUCING GENERIC SCOPE

We have noted earlier that generics (e.g., "Why do you think only *men* can be race car drivers?") are a frequent means of referring to gender categories, and that children produce about as many generics as mothers at each age. These patterns raise the question of who is leading the way in generic talk: mothers or children? Does one speaker or the other predominantly shift the conversation from discussion of individuals to discussion of the larger category? The analyses conducted earlier examine only relative frequency of generic talk, but not who initiates generic talk. To examine this question, we conducted a page-by-page analysis of the use of generics. For this analysis, we focused only on generics that explicitly used a noun or pronoun to refer to a person. For each page in the picture book for which at least one generic was produced, we examined who produced a generic first (mother or child), and also whether or not the other speaker also contributed a generic. This resulted in each page being coded into one of five mutually exclusive categories: (a) Only the mother produced a generic; (b) The mother produced a generic first, then the child produced a generic, too; (c) Only the child produced a generic; (d) The child produced a generic first, then the mother produced a generic, too; (e) No generics were produced. If mothers are leading the way in the use of generics, and children simply following the path set by mothers, then we should see primarily patterns (a) and (b). However, if children are also actively producing generics, then we should also see substantial amounts of patterns (c) and (d). Only categories (a) through (d) were analyzed further.

We summed the number of pages of each type (a, b, c, or d, above) for those pages on which at least one generic was produced, broken down by the gendered activity of the page. For example, chopping wood was considered a male activity (regardless of whether a man or a woman was shown chopping wood); playing with dolls was considered a female activity (regardless of whether a boy or a girl was shown playing with dolls). Pages on which no generics were produced were scored as 0. Altogether, scores could range from 0 to 12 per activity-gender (i.e., 12 male-activity pages, 12 female-activity pages). We conducted a 3 (age group: 2, 4, 6) × 2 (child sex: boy, girl), by 2 (activity gender: male, female) × 2 (generic-first: mother, child) × 2 (number of generic speakers: 1, 2) ANOVA. Age group and child sex were between-subjects factors, and activity gender, generic-first, and number of generic speakers were within-subjects variables.

We found a generic-first × number of speakers interaction, $F(1, 66) = 34.62$, $p < .001$, $\eta^2 = .34$. When mothers introduced generics first, they typically were the only speaker contributing generics (one speaker more often than two speakers, $p < .001$), whereas when children introduced generics first, they more typically were followed in by the mother (instead of being the only speaker contributing generics; two speakers more often than one speaker, $p < .01$). See Table 14. This result suggests that mothers overall were more responsive to children than vice versa, continuing with generics when they were introduced by their children.

The patterns interacted with age, however. There was a main effect of age, $F(2, 66) = 16.15$, $p < .001$, $\eta^2 = .33$, indicating that generics increased dramatically in frequency from 2 years to 4 and 6 years of age ($M = 5.79$, 13.34, and 15.21 pages out of 24, respectively, including at least one generic; $SD = 4.18$, 7.53, and 5.64; 2's differed from 4's and 6's, $p < .001$). Age also interacted with the generic-first factor, $F(2, 66) = 5.51$, $p < .01$, $\eta^2 = .14$. The rate at which mothers introduced generics first did not significantly vary by age ($M = 4.71$, 5.38, and 5.79, $SD = 3.44$, 4.11, and 4.00, at ages 2, 4, and 6, respectively), whereas the rate at which children introduced generics

TABLE 14

MEAN NUMBER OF PAGES (OUT OF 24 POSSIBLE) ON WHICH EITHER CHILD OR MOTHER
INTRODUCED A GENERIC, AS A FUNCTION OF NUMBER OF SPEAKERS PRODUCING GENERICS

	Overall	Age 2	Age 4	Age 6
Mother introduces generic, no child generic:	3.79 (3.13)	4.38 (3.03)	3.62 (3.42)	3.38 (2.97)
Mother introduces generic, child follows in:	1.50 (2.02)	0.33 (1.05)	1.75 (1.65)	2.42 (2.53)
Child introduces generic, no mother generic:	2.18 (3.55)	0.33 (0.76)	2.08 (2.80)	4.12 (4.80)
Child introduces generic, mother follows in:	3.97 (5.15)	0.75 (1.85)	5.88 (6.23)	5.29 (4.83)

Note.—SDs are in parentheses.

first increased significantly with age ($M = 1.08$, 7.96, and 9.42 pages per book, at ages 2, 4, and 6, respectively; $SD = 2.45$, 7.66, and 6.61; 2's differed from 4's and 6's, $p < .005$). Also interacting with age was the number of speakers using a generic, $F(2, 66) = 4.05$, $p < .05$, $\eta^2 = .11$. In conversations with 2-year-olds, 81% of the time that generics were used, they were used by one speaker only (primarily mothers, as seen above) (i.e., at age 2, generics were more often used by one speaker than by both speakers, $p < .02$), whereas this rate decreased to 43% in conversations with 4-year-olds, and 49% in conversations with 6-year-olds (i.e., at ages 4 and 6, generics were as likely to be used by both speakers as by just one speaker).

The remaining effects involved activity gender. There was an activity-gender × generic-first interaction, $F(1, 66) = 9.41$, $p < .01$, $\eta^2 = .12$. Children introduced generics first more often for male than for female activities, whereas mothers introduced generics first more often for female than male activities, $p < .05$. There was also an activity-gender × number-of-speakers interaction, $F(1, 66) = 9.91$, $p < .01$, $\eta^2 = .13$. This indicates a greater involvement of both speakers when discussing male vs. female activities, and a greater involvement of just one speaker when discussing female vs. male activities, $p < .05$, Bonferroni. These interactions are depicted in Figure 19.

Summary

At 2 years of age, generics are primarily introduced by the mother. However, at both 4 and 6 years of age, children are actually introducing generics more often than mothers. Thus, children's focus on category-wide generalizations seems often spontaneous, by the time they reach 4 years of age. The dramatic change between 2 and 4 years is of interest, and helps explain the finding reported earlier, that conversations with 2-year-olds include generics so much less often than conversations with older children.

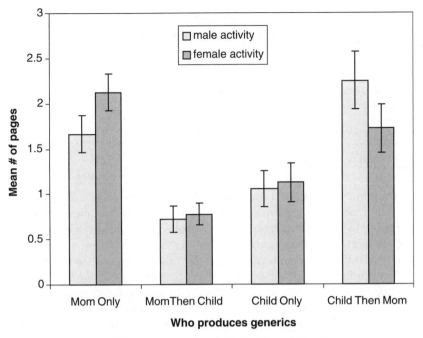

Note: Vertical bars depict standard errors of the means.

FIGURE 19.—Mean number of pages on which generics are produced, as a function of number of speakers producing a generic (1 or 2), which participant introduces generic first (mother or child), and activity type (male or female).

Recall that at 2 years of age, generics are much less frequent both among children and among their mothers. The current analyses suggest that mothers of 2-year-olds are attempting to use generics, but (a) rarely see them spontaneously in their own children's expression, and (b) rarely have them followed up by their children. These findings suggest that the developmental changes in generic use taking place between 2 and 4 years of age may be primarily due to changes in the children.

MOTHER–CHILD CORRELATIONS IN SPEECH

How close a correspondence can be found between mother and child talk about gender? To examine this question, we looked at correspondences between mothers and children on each of the major descriptive categories analyzed in Chapter III (stereotype affirmations, generics, gender-ostensive labeling, gender contrasts, and equality statements). Specifically, we conducted partial correlations between the frequency of child utterances

85

TABLE 15

PARTIAL CORRELATIONS BETWEEN MOTHER AND CHILD SPEECH, CONTROLLING
FOR CHILD AGE GROUP

Variable	Correlation	N	p-Value
Affirm gender stereotypes	.09	72	n.s.
Negate gender stereotypes	.23	72	= .056
Generics	.48	72	< .001
Gender-ostensive labeling	.78	72	< .001
Gender contrasts	.53	72	< .001
Gender equality statements	.63	72	< .001

and frequency of maternal utterances of a given type, controlling for age. (In each case, the frequencies were divided by the number of on-task utterances by the speaker, so as to control for overall differences across dyads in degree of talkativeness.) These analyses provide a first look at the stability of individual differences in gender talk across mother–child dyads.

The findings are presented in Table 15. As can be seen, mothers and children did not correspond in the amount of stereotype affirmations. They showed a non-significant tendency to correlate with one another in stereotype negations. In all other respects that were examined, there was quite close correspondence between mothers and children: in generics, gender-ostensive labeling, gender contrasts, and equality statements. Mothers who use many generics tend to have children who use many generics; mothers who engage in frequent gender-ostensive labeling tend to have children who engage in frequent gender-ostensive labeling, etc. Furthermore, the correlations are quite high, ranging from .48 (generics) to .78 (gender-ostensive labeling).

The extent of these correlations is intriguing, although they raise more questions than they answer. We cannot determine *why* mothers and children look so much alike in their talk. One possibility is that these differences are an artifact of the conversation itself—that is, perhaps being in conversation with a speaker who sets the agenda leads to a spurious correlation between the two speakers. However, it is also possible that these differences reflect stable differences that would arise even if the members of the dyad were talking with other people. From the present study, we cannot untangle these possibilities. However, the data are certainly deserving of follow-up research.

CORRELATIONS BETWEEN TALK AND GENDER-TYPING MEASURES

Children

Here we examine how children's talk corresponds to their gender knowledge and flexibility (as measured on the gender-typing and gender

TABLE 16

DESCRIPTIVE STATISTICS CONCERNING CHILD MEASURES OF GENDER-TYPING AND
GENDER CONSTANCY

	Mean	(SD)	Comparison to Chance	Cronbach's α	Total # Items
Labeling					
Age 2	12.92	(3.19)	$t(23) = 7.55, p < .001$	.81	16
Gender flexibility ("both")					
Age 4	7.42	(3.98)	$t(23) = 2.57, p < .02$	.81	16
Age 6	8.96	(3.52)	$t(23) = 5.04, p < .001$	.76	16
Gender constancy—self					
Age 2	4.25	(1.67)	$t(23) = 3.66, p < .001$	.70	6
Age 4	5.67	(0.70)	$t(23) = 18.61, p < .001$	.48	6
Age 6	5.87	(0.34)	$t(23) = 41.69, p < .001$	.00	6
Gender constancy—other					
Age 4	7.00	(1.10)	$t(23) = 13.32, p < .001$	.37	8
Age 6	7.62	(0.65)	$t(23) = 27.45, p < .001$	.27	8

constancy tasks). Specifically, we ask whether talk during the book-reading task predicts other, more standard measures in the literature. The independent variables included child age and children's scores on the six primary book-reading variables: stereotype affirmations, stereotype negations, generics, gender ostensive labeling, gender contrast, and gender equality. The dependent measures were as follows (see Table 16 for descriptive statistics on each of these measures):

Gender flexibility (4- and 6-year-olds)

This task included 16 gender-stereotyped items (4 each for boy, girl, man, and woman) and 4 gender-neutral items. The gender-neutral items were included only for the sake of including variation in the stimulus set, and were not analyzed further. Each child received a single score, potentially ranging from 0 to 16, indicating the number of trials on which they said that *both* males and females could engage in a gender-stereotyped activity. (Two-year-olds were not given the option of answering that both sexes could engage in an activity, and therefore were not included in the analyses.)

Gender constancy: self (2-, 4-, and 6-year-olds)

As a reminder, these were the questions about whether the child had been and would be of the same gender category over time. We summed the

87

number of trials on which each child endorsed the gender-constant response, yielding a score potentially ranging from 0 to 6.

Gender constancy: other (4- and 6-year-olds only)

On this task, children saw a picture of a baby in a diaper, were told its gender (boy or girl), and then were asked a series of questions regarding whether the child would change gender if he/she wore clothes appropriate to the other sex, and if he/she changed back into his/her regular clothes. We coded responses to the two key questions: "What does X look like, a boy or a girl?" and "What is X really, a boy or a girl?" Each question was asked after the initial transformation and again after the baby was changed back into regular clothes, for each of two different items (a boy and a girl item), yielding a total of eight questions (2 questions × 2 transformations × 2 items). Correct responses to these eight questions were summed.

For each of the three child measures (gender flexibility, gender constancy (self), and gender constancy (other)), we conducted linear regressions using the stepwise method. For the gender flexibility task, stereotype negation during the picture-book session was the only significant predictor variable, $\beta = .42$, $p < .005$, adjusted $R^2 = .16$, $F(1, 46) = 9.86$, $p < .005$. For the gender constancy (self) task, significant predictor variables were age group ($\beta = .39$, $p = .001$) and stereotype affirmations during book reading ($\beta = .29$, $p = .01$), adjusted $R^2 = .32$, $F(2, 69) = 17.82$, $p < .001$. For the gender constancy (other) task, age group was the only significant predictor variable, $\beta = .13$, $p < .05$, $R^2 = .11$, $F(1, 46) = 5.73$, $p < .05$.

These analyses suggest that children's gender-relevant talk during the book-reading task correlates with more standard measures outside the book-reading context: gender-stereotype flexibility as measured on an experimental task and gender constancy of the self. Children's talk is therefore a fairly direct expression of their gender concepts.

Mothers

Here we examine how mothers' talk corresponds to their gender typing (as measured by personal endorsement of gender-typed properties, and by attitudes toward gender-typed properties). As with the analyses of children above, we ask whether talk during the book-reading task predicts other, more standard measures in the literature. The independent variables included child age and mothers' scores on the six primary book-reading variables: stereotype affirmations, stereotype negations, generics, gender ostensive labeling, gender contrast, and gender equality. The dependent

TABLE 17

DESCRIPTIVE STATISTICS CONCERNING MATERNAL GENDER-TYPING MEASURES

	Mean	(SD)	Comparison to Chance	Cronbach's α	Total # Items
Attitude measures—mean % "both" responses					
Female items	.80	(.22)	$t(71) = 11.60, p < .001$	.94	36
Male items	.84	(.21)	$t(71) = 14.05, p < .001$	.94	35
Personal measures—scale score[a]					
Female items	2.61	(0.24)	$t(71) = 13.44, p < .001$	.73	34
Male items	2.16	(0.30)	$t(71) = 23.77, p < .001$	.82	37

[a]Scale scores range from 1 = not at all (occupations); not at all like me (trait); never (activity) to 4 = very much (occupation); very much like me (trait); often or very often (activity).

measures were as follows (see Table 17 for descriptive statistics on each of these measures):

Attitude measures

These included mothers' attitudes of how appropriate each of the occupations, activities, and traits were to men or women more generally ("Who should…?"). We excluded from analysis all gender-neutral items. From the remaining 71 items, we created two composite scores, one for "feminine" items ($N = 36$) and one for "masculine" items ($N = 35$). For each, we summed the number of items on which each mother said that both men and women should X (i.e., indicated as 3 on the 5-point scale), and divided by the total number of items (see Liben & Bigler, 2002). This provides a measure of gender-stereotype flexibility. Occasionally mothers would skip items; such trials were subtracted from the item total in these calculations (e.g., a mother who said "both" on 68 trials, and who skipped 3 items, received a score of 100%). Scores across individuals ranged considerably, from a low of 32% to a high of 100%.

Personal measures

These included mothers' assessment of how relevant or desirable each of the occupations, activities, and traits were to themselves. We excluded from analysis all gender-neutral items. From the remaining 71 items, we created two composite scores: one averaging mothers' responses to the "feminine" items ($N = 34$), and one averaging mothers' responses to the "masculine" items ($N = 37$), all on a 4-point scale (see Liben & Bigler, 2002). This provides measures of mothers' gender-typing of the self, for feminine and masculine attributes separately.

89

For each of the four maternal gender-typing measures (personal endorsement (female), personal endorsement (male), attitudes (female), and attitudes (male)), we conducted linear regressions using the stepwise method. For personal endorsement of female properties (paper-and-pencil task), gender contrasts during book-reading provided the only significant predictor variable, $\beta = .28$, $p < .02$, adjusted $R^2 = .07$, $F(1, 70) = 6.08$, $p < .02$. For personal endorsement of male properties (paper-and-pencil task), the only significant predictor variable was age group ($\beta = .28$, $p = .02$), adjusted $R^2 = .06$, $F(1, 70) = 5.96$, $p < .02$. There were no significant predictors for either gender attitudes (male) or gender attitudes (female).

These analyses suggest that one aspect of mothers' gender-relevant talk during the book-reading task (namely, gender contrasts) correlates with a more standard measure outside the book-reading context (personal endorsement of female properties). Mothers who explicitly contrast male with female (an implicit way of accentuating gender categories) are those who perceive themselves as more "feminine" on a variety of characteristics: they self-identified with female occupations, activities, and traits.

SUMMARY AND DISCUSSION

Understanding the nature of parent–child conversations about gender cannot be accomplished wholly by examining the speech of each participant separately or in isolation. Certain revealing patterns can be observed only by documenting the discourse patterns in the conversation as a whole, and by comparing such speech to other measures. Specifically, this chapter examined three core questions: (1) How often do mothers support or reject their children's expression of gender stereotypes? (2) Who typically initiates talk about general *categories* of people (including gender categories)—mothers or children? (3) How closely does talk during the book-reading task correspond to gender beliefs and attitudes, as measured by gender-typing and gender-constancy tasks? We discuss each of these questions in turn.

How Often Do Mothers Support or Reject Their Children's Expression of Gender Stereotypes?

For this question, it is not clear what one would predict based on past research. On the one hand, prior studies have repeatedly found that parents encourage gender-stereotyped play and toy preferences, and discourage cross-gender play and toy preferences, from when their children are young (e.g., Eisenberg et al., 1985; Fagot, 1978; Fagot et al., 1985; Lytton & Romney, 1991). Therefore, we might expect to see mothers' active encouragement and approval of children's expression of gender stereotypes. On the other hand, the mothers in this sample show no tendency to express gender stereotypes themselves, and typically express highly flexible attitudes, when asked whether various occupations, activities, and traits are more appropriate for men or women. Furthermore, children's expressions of gender stereotypes were often quite blatant (e.g., "Because ballet dancers are girls!"). Therefore, we might expect to see mothers discouraging their children from expressing gender stereotypes.

When we look at the sequential and contingent patterns of talk, we find that mothers are surprisingly accepting of children's stereotyping statements (particularly those that are stated in positive, rather than negative terms). Mothers rarely directly contradicted a child's gender stereotype statement, and in fact more often affirmed the child's stereotype than questioned it. However, where we did see more resistance from mothers was when children expressed a stereotype in terms of what someone or some people *can't*, *don't*, or *shouldn't* do (vs. what someone or some people can, do, or should do). For example, the statement that boys play with trucks would lead to little comment from the mother, whereas the statement that girls *can't* play with trucks would more likely be disputed or questioned.

Who Initiates Talk About General Categories of People (i.e., Generics)—Mothers or Children?

The answer to this question depends on the age of the child. In conversations with 2-year-olds, mothers were more likely to initiate talk about generic categories than were their children. However, by 4 years of age there was a marked shift, and children primarily initiated talk about generic categories. A sharp developmental increase between 2 and 4 years of age in children's talk about generic categories has also been found in prior studies not focused on gender per see (Gelman, 2003). Perhaps part of the developmental change in children's attention to gender follows from more general changes in children's categorization and cognitive functioning (see also Maccoby, 1988). There is a rich variety of evidence demonstrating that young children and even infants are capable of categorizing themselves and others on the basis of gender (e.g., Katz, 1996; Leinbach & Fagot, 1993; Poulin-Dubois, Serbin, Kenyon, & Derbyshire, 1994; Levy & Haaf, 1994; see Martin, Rubin, & Szkrybalo, 2002, and Powlishta, Sen, Serbin, Poulin-Dubois, & Eichstedt, 2001, for a review). Despite this early capacity to attend to gender, there appear to be changes with age in the *salience* of gender categories. Maccoby (1998) proposes that children's sense of gender group identity and own-sex biases are likely to become progressively more important as children move from preschool to elementary school. Perhaps children's increasing attention to general categories (vs. individuals) also contributes to this change.

How Closely Does Talk During the Book-Reading Task Correspond to
Gender Beliefs and Attitudes, as Measured by Gender-Typing and
Gender-Constancy Tasks?

Altogether, there are a few sensible correlations between the gender-type measures and the picture-book task, for both mothers and children. These results suggest that implicit messages conveyed in parent–child conversations may reflect individual differences in beliefs about gender. However, it is important to note that the order of the tasks may have influenced how mothers and children responded on the tasks, as the tasks were presented in fixed order (the gender-typing and gender-constancy tasks always came directly after the picture-book reading task). For example, the picture book included various stereotyped and counter-stereotyped characters, and so may have highlighted or primed certain ways of thinking about gender. Likewise, parental talk during the book session may have influenced children's judgments. We made sure that the items children received in the gender-typing task did not overlap with any of the items in the picture book. Thus, cross-task correlations could not be a result of specific content conveyed during book-reading. Nonetheless, there may have been carryover from the book-reading task, so correlations that were obtained need to be interpreted cautiously.

Interestingly, individual differences in maternal speech about gender strikingly predict individual differences in child speech about gender. This result also must be interpreted cautiously, because the shared interaction may have created the mother–child correlations (i.e., such correlations may not persist when mothers and children are talking to people other than one another). Nonetheless, the result raises the possibility that ways of articulating gender may be transmitted from mothers to children, such that a mother's relative (implicit) focus on gender gets conveyed to her child.

NOTES

9. Most maternal responses received a single code, but occasionally responses received two codes, for example, Affirm and Question. The Other response was used only for codes that did not fall into another category. Therefore, if a mother gave an affirmation plus other information that did not fit into one of the pre-existing codes, that was coded only as an affirmation.

10. Yule's Q is a conservative measure of contingency that takes into account the base-rate probability of each component in a sequence (see Bakeman & Gottman, 1997, p. 129, though note that the formula presented in this edition contains an error; the correct formula is $[ad - bc]/[ad + bc]$). The Yule's Q score ranges from -1 to $+1$, with 0 indicating no effect.

VI. GENERAL DISCUSSION

One of the most salient and important social categories throughout the lifespan is that of gender. As years of research have documented, gender is prominent beginning early in childhood: infants attend to gender, toddlers label people on the basis of gender by 2 or 2-1/2 years of age, and gender categories guide children's behaviors and stereotyping throughout the preschool years and beyond. Children's gender concepts and gender stereotyping also undergo rapid increases in the early years, with dramatic changes in gender constancy and gender-related knowledge between two and six years of age. Furthermore, children *essentialize* gender by treating categories of male and female as biologically based, mutually exclusive, opposite to one another, and reflective of deep, non-obvious, immutable differences (Gelman & Taylor, 2000; Bohan, 1993; see review in Chapter I).

Researchers agree that children's gender concepts are unlikely to be wholly self-generated, and instead are open to cultural and environmental influences. Yet to this point little is known about how parents and children *talk* about gender in their everyday conversations. The present study was designed to examine parent–child conversations about gender to address two sets of questions: What can we learn about children's early gender beliefs from their talk? and, What kinds of information do mothers provide to their children in ordinary speech? Below we address what these data suggest about children's concepts and about maternal input. But first we summarize several central points regarding the data as a whole.

CONVERSATIONS AS A WHOLE

Explicit vs. Implicit Focus on Gender

One of the most important findings of this study was the contrast between explicit and implicit talk about gender. What we are calling "explicit" talk about gender includes those statements regarding what people can, do, should, or like to do, with regard to the gender-stereotyped activities and occupations that were the focus of the picture book. These include gender-stereotyping statements (e.g., "Boys don't ever be ballet dancers" [girl, age 6.5 years]), anti-stereotyping statements (e.g., "Maybe Daddy" [does dusting; girl, age 2.69]), utterances that refer to gender but don't take a stance one way or another (e.g., "Can mommies be race-car drivers?" [mother of a 2-year-old boy]), and utterances that by-pass the dimension of gender altogether (e.g., "And grown-ups" [help bake cookies]; boy, age 4.45). In their *explicit* talk about gender stereotypes, children were much more gender-typed than their mothers, who were equally likely to deny as to affirm the traditional pairings of gender and activity.

In contrast, what we are calling *implicit* talk about gender includes a variety of other, more subtle ways of emphasizing gender categories. These include references to the *category* of gender by means of generic noun phrases (e.g., "Do bigger boys play with dolls?"), gender-ostensive labeling (e.g., "That is a lady sewing a dress, right?"), errors in references to counter-stereotypical pictures (e.g., "a man" referring to a woman driving a truck), and gender contrasts (e.g., "Is that a boy or a girl?"; "Do you think that's more of a girl job or a boy job?"). Implicit talk about gender was highly frequent, especially among mothers: during the book-reading task, 64% of mothers made a gender contrast at least once, 89% of mothers engaged in gender-ostensive labeling at least once, and 96% of mothers used generics at least once. Nearly half of all person references provided by mothers made explicit mention of gender with either gendered pronouns (e.g., "his") or gendered nouns (e.g., "man") (compared to only 24% making explicit mention of age). Furthermore, even when we focus just on person-referring *nouns* (where mothers have the choice of invoking gender or not), over 60% mark gender.

The contrast between explicit vs. implicit talk may have implications for data and arguments that parents play a minimal role during gender social-ization. Lytton and Romney (1991) conducted a meta-analysis of 172 studies and found that most studies of parent socializing effects find non-significant and very small effect sizes. The socialization areas that were examined in-cluded: amount of interaction; total achievement encouragement; warmth, nurturance, and responsiveness; encouragement of dependency; restric-tiveness/low encouragement of independence; disciplinary strictness; en-couragement of gender-typed activities; gender-typed perception; and clarity of communication/use of reasoning. However, the present data sug-gest that gender socializing may exist in subtle aspects of language that would not have been measured in past research. This suggestion thus sup-ports Leaper's (2002) proposal that fine-grained analyses may be critical, if one is to detect parental influences on children's gender development.

At times the explicit and implicit talk presented conflicting messag-es—perhaps because speakers are more consciously aware of the messages they present explicitly than those they present implicitly. First, mothers were more neutral or gender-egalitarian than children in explicit stereotyping statements, but were just as likely as the children to produce implicit talk about gender, including generics, gender-ostensive labeling, and gender contrasts. A second example concerns a bias in explicit statements toward stereotyping of *females*, but a bias in implicit statements toward stereotyping of *males,* in particular for generics and gender-ostensive labeling. Third, when encountering gender-inconsistent pages, dyads produced explicit statements that were *more egalitarian*, but also demonstrated a *greater implicit focus on gender* (more generics, ostensive labeling, and contrasts). Finally, although 2-year-olds displayed no awareness of gender stereotypes in their explicit statements about gendered activities, they revealed implicit awareness of gender stereotypes in their naming errors (distorting labels to conform to stereotypic expectations; e.g., referring to a woman firefighter as a man).

The finding of a distinction between implicit and explicit talk about gender fits with recent work showing that adults display a distinction between explicit and implicit gender stereotypes or attitudes (Lemm & Banaji, 1999). Explicit gender stereotypes and attitudes are typically assessed by verbal self-report measures (e.g., "Do you agree that men and women ought to have equal opportunities for employment?"), whereas implicit gender stereotypes and attitudes can be assessed by means of response speed on a simple judgment task (e.g., how quickly a participant judges that "John" is male, when following the word "delicate" vs. when following the word "rough"; Blair & Banaji, 1996; see also Greenwald & Banaji, 1995). Interestingly, implicit and explicit attitudes about gender can differ in strength and direction (Lemm & Banaji, 1999). For example, participants' explicit attitudes toward women in leadership roles (e.g., managers, politicians) were by-and-large unrelated to their implicit attitudes. Lemm and Banaji suggest that implicit attitudes and beliefs are held at an unconscious level, with only tangential links to measures that rely on consciously accessed judgments.

The following three exchanges illustrate the contrast between explicit and implicit talk about gender in our data. The first example is of a mother who explicitly embraces a counter-stereotypical example (expressing positive attitudes about a woman being a firefighter), but also emphasizes her gender (by means of gender-ostensive labeling), and highlights that it is unusual (the child, a son, is 6.96 years old; gender-stereotype negations and gender-ostensive labeling are marked in pointed brackets):

Mother: You know what?
Mother: I notice something really different about this firefighter.
           ⟨Negate Stereotype⟩

Child:	A girl. ⟨Label⟩
Mother:	Yeah, it is a girl. ⟨Label⟩
Mother:	How do you know that?
Child:	Her hair is longer.
Mother:	Yeah, what else?
Child:	It doesn't look like a boy. ⟨Label⟩
Mother:	It doesn't look like a boy. ⟨Label⟩
Mother:	Look at her lips.
Mother:	Does she look like she has lipstick on?
Child:	Mm-hm [yes]
Mother:	Mm.
Mother:	She almost looks... what? [pointing to her tummy]
Mother:	Pregnant. [laughs]
Mother:	To me, but they wouldn't let a pregnant person be a firefighter probably. ⟨Affirm Stereotype⟩
Mother:	But it's probably just that big coat she's wearing.
Mother:	So that's neat, a firefighter being a woman. ⟨Label⟩ ⟨Negate Stereotype⟩
Mother:	Cool.

In the next two examples, the mother takes her child's statements about *specific* individuals who can or cannot do a particular activity, and moves the child toward a discussion of *generic* gender categories. The first example is from a conversation between a mother and her son, age 2.8 years, as they look at a picture of a boy playing football (individual and generic person scope references are marked in pointed brackets):

Mother:	Is this a boy or a girl? ⟨Individual⟩
Child:	Boy. ⟨Individual⟩
Mother:	A boy? ⟨Individual⟩
Mother:	Can girls play football? ⟨Generic⟩
Child:	No.

In the following example, the mother probes to see if her daughter's aversion to driving a truck has a gendered basis, taking what was initially expressed as an individual preference (on the part of the child; a girl 6.31 years of age) and turning it into an expression of a more general gendered attitude. Note that the mother never herself expresses the attitude that driving trucks is just for boys, but her move from individual to generic suggests this possibility. The excerpt comes toward the end of a conversation about who drives trucks (individual and generic person scope references are marked in pointed brackets):

96

Mother:	You don't think you'd look cool driving a truck? ⟨Individual⟩
Child:	No.
Mother:	No?
Mother:	You'd look cool driving a convertible? ⟨Individual⟩
Child:	Yeah.
Mother:	[laughs] Yeah.
Child:	I'll look like an idiot driving a truck. ⟨Individual⟩
Mother:	Why do you think so?
Mother:	What, you think you'll look like a boy? ⟨Individual⟩
Child:	No.
Mother:	Why would you look like an idiot driving a truck? ⟨Individual⟩
Child:	Because I just don't like trucks. ⟨Individual⟩
Mother:	You don't like trucks. ⟨Individual⟩
Mother:	You think most girls don't like trucks? ⟨Generic⟩
Child:	Yeah.
Mother:	Why?
Child:	I don't know.
Child:	Let's just get on.
Mother:	Okay.
Mother:	Why, because it's associated with work?
Child:	Here [helping mom turn page]
Mother:	Or boys? ⟨Generic⟩
Mother:	Is it 'cause boys drive trucks that you don't want to drive one? ⟨Generic [boys]⟩ ⟨Individual [you]⟩
Child:	Yeah.

One of the major findings was that generics are a frequent form of reference to gender, and that they show distinctive patterns of use. All but 3 of the mothers in our sample (96%) used generics at least once in the conversation, as did 72% of the children, ranging from less than a third of the 2-year-olds, to over 90% of the 4- and 6-year-olds. Generics differ from non-generics in scope (generics were broader in scope), content (generics were more male-biased than non-generics, and also more likely to refer to a non-gendered referent), form (generics were more likely to be gendered), and modality (with generics relatively more focused on *can* and *should* than non-generics). Finally, mothers were less likely to affirm children's *generic* stereotyping statements (e.g., "Boys" [can fix a bicycle]) than to their *non-generic* stereotyping statements (e.g., "Dad can" [be a racecar driver]). Generics are thus an important and distinctive means of highlighting the salience of gender categories.

Generics are of particular interest because they embody much of what we mean by "gender essentialism." Consider the following excerpt from a paper by Bohan (1993, p. 9):

The experiences attributed to women, portrayed as contributing to their "nature," are not timeless and universal but are socially, historically, and politically located; essentialist models fail to acknowledge this situatedness... To presume that all women judge, think, or relate in a characteristic and universal manner denies the contextuality that, as psychologists, we know frames behavior.

What is intriguing here is that generics—like essentialist models: (a) characterize gender in a universal manner and (b) abstract away from any particular or situated context. Whereas specific nouns can refer to particular points in time or space, generics cannot. Boys play with trucks; Ballet dancers are girls—these are statements that characterize a gender category as timeless, universal, and devoid of context.

Conversations with Girls vs. Conversations with Boys

Although the patterns of talk with girls and with boys were comparable in many ways, there were also some consistent differences depending on the sex of the child. Most notably, conversations with girls focused more on females, and conversations with boys focused more on males. This finding is sensible, given that participants often talked about themselves (e.g., "I don't, I can't play with dolls"), which by necessity would render an own-sex bias. More interestingly, girls provided more gender-neutral talk than boys, which can be attributed to a greater focus among girls than boys on non-gendered categories (most typically those based on age, but also occupations and ethnicity). It appears that, whereas boys primarily talk about activities in terms of gender, girls more readily construe the activities in terms of other dimensions besides gender. This result suggests that boys may be more likely to invoke gender as an organizing principle for taking in information. This finding is consistent with prior work showing that girls tend to interpret gender-neutral language (e.g., "they," "the student") as more gender-inclusive than boys, that is, girls are more likely to interpret such expressions as including female referents (Gastil, 1990; Henley, 1989; Switzer, 1990). These gender differences would be interesting to explore in more depth, using non-language tasks. For example, when given a non-linguistic sorting task in which people can be sorted along multiple dimensions, does gender get used more often by boys than by girls?

The finding that boys have more powerful gender schemas than girls is consistent with a variety of research that has found that boys are more likely than girls to maintain gender boundaries (see Leaper, 2000, p. 143, for a review). For example, third- and fourth-grade boys reject cross-sex behavior more than do girls (Bussey & Perry, 1982). Similarly, in a study of preadolescents attending a summer day camp, Sroufe, Bennett, Englund,

Urban, and Shulman (1993) found that boys were more vigilant about actively defining gender boundaries than girls (e.g., expressing dislike of girls, or leaving an area where girls can be found), though boys were also more likely to violate gender boundaries (e.g., by hovering or flirting). Moreover, boys typically receive more negative consequences from parents for violating gender stereotypes than do girls (Fagot, 1977; Thorne & Luria, 1986).

Leaper (2000) suggests that these gender differences fit with social identity theory, which predicts that those in high-status groups will work harder to maintain group boundaries than those in low-status groups. Mahalingam (1998) reports a similar effect in India with adults: members of a high-caste group tend to essentialize caste (reporting that it is inborn and unmalleable), whereas members of a low-caste group tend to treat caste as socially constructed. Our findings are consistent with these claims, and suggest further that gender may be relatively more *salient* to boys than girls (i.e., boys invoke gender boundaries and gender categories more often than girls).

A further sex difference was that boys provided more negative-valence talk than girls—that is, more talk about what people *cannot* (or do not, should not, etc.) do. This was quite a sizeable effect, with more than twice as many negative-valence utterances from boys than from girls (although, it should be noted, negative-valence utterances were infrequent overall). There are several possible sources of this effect. Perhaps boys are more negative in general, less eager to please, and/or more free to speak their mind (Whiting & Edwards, 1988). However, another intriguing possibility is that this finding may reflect a greater concern among boys regarding the boundaries on male and female behavior (see Leaper, 2000). In other words, if violations of gender stereotypes are more threatening to boys than girls, and if boys are especially focused on "policing" gender boundaries, then they may often talk about what people *cannot* do. Here is an example of the sort of conversation involving negative-valence utterances from a boy, age 4.97 (coding of valence appears in pointed brackets):

Mother:	"Who can be a sailor?"
Child:	[shakes head "no" at picture of woman sailor] ⟨Negative Valence⟩
Mother:	Why not?
Child:	[shakes head "no"]
Mother:	Mm.
Mother:	Do you think she'd be a good sailor or a bad sailor? ⟨Question Valence⟩
Child:	[whispers] Bad. ⟨Negative Valence⟩
Mother:	What was that?

Child:	[whispers] Bad ⟨Negative Valence⟩
Mother:	Say it louder.
Child:	[whispers] Bad. ⟨Negative Valence⟩
Mother:	Bad? ⟨Question Valence⟩
Child:	[nods "yes"] ⟨Negative Valence⟩
Mother:	Why would she be a bad sailor? ⟨Negative Valence⟩
Child:	Because she would blown over and fall under the water. ⟨Negative Valence⟩
Mother:	No, no she wouldn't. ⟨Positive Valence⟩

This emphasis on what is *not* appropriate is a particularly powerful means of expressing gender stereotypes, compared to statements about who *can* do certain activities.

Talk about Males vs. Talk about Females

Males and females are talked about in different ways. Across the various analyses, there are three noteworthy patterns. First, as already noted, there was an own-sex bias in the conversations. We can see this in expression of attitudes toward gender-stereotyped activities, where conversations with boys included more talk about males, and conversations with girls included more talk about females.

The second pattern involving sex-of-referent was a detectable male bias, which arose both in generics (slightly more common in reference to males than in reference to females) and in gender-ostensive labeling (again, more common regarding males than females). This male bias makes sense for two reasons: stereotypes for males are culturally more powerful (Hort et al., 1990), and males tend to be the unmarked or default category (Waugh, 1982).

Finally, there was also a third pattern, though this one was entirely unexpected. Namely, there was a female bias overall, when it came to affirming gender stereotypes. Why was there more stereotyping of females than of males? This result is at first surprising, given that past work has found that males are more tightly restricted in their roles—for example, it is more negatively viewed for a boy to wear a skirt than for a girl to wear a tie. We would have predicted, therefore, the reverse pattern: greater stereotyping of males than of females. However, it is important to recall that the effect was carried by the girls (and their mothers). In other words, girls—not boys—stereotyped females more than males. This pattern seems to reflect a bias for children to stereotype their own gender more rigidly. And in fact, boys did stereotype males more than females—a finding consistent with this interpretation. A further potentially relevant factor may be the gender make-up of the dyads. 75% of the participants were females: half of the children, and all of the mothers. This preponderance of females may have also contributed to a bias to focus on females. Availability of the mother as an exemplar may have upped the number of female stereotyping statements.

Page Differences: Gender-Consistent vs. Gender-Inconsistent

As noted earlier, we found that speakers talked quite differently about gender when looking at pages that depicted gender-consistent activities (e.g., girl playing with doll) vs. pages that depicted gender-inconsistent activities (e.g., boy playing with doll). When looking at gender-inconsistent pages, speakers were more likely to express counter-stereotypical attitudes (e.g., "A dad" [can knit a sweater]), and to provide gender-ostensive labeling (e.g., "This is a him"), gender contrasts (e.g., "Boys [can be a cheerleader], but mostly girls do it"), and gender equality statements (e.g., "Every grown-up in the world" [can be a sailor]). Furthermore, mothers were more likely to provide generics on gender-inconsistent pages (e.g., "Did you know girls can chop trees down?"). The following example, between a mother and her daughter, age 4.87 years, illustrates how the counter-stereotyping picture can be used to persuade a child to accept a counter-stereotypical possibility (coding of attitude toward the gender-stereotype is indicated in pointed brackets):

Mother:	Do you think George[11] could grow up to be a ballet dancer? ⟨Question Stereotype⟩
Child:	No. ⟨Affirm Stereotype⟩
Mother:	No? ⟨Question Stereotype⟩
Mother:	Why not?
Child:	No. [overlapping with line above.] ⟨Affirm Stereotype⟩
Child:	Because he's a boy.
Mother:	This shows a boy who's doing ballet. ⟨Negate Stereotype⟩
Child:	Oh, so boys can, but girls can. [The word "but" here is interesting, suggesting that it would have been more normative to have a boy/girl contrast.] ⟨Negate stereotype [boys can]⟩ ⟨Affirm stereotype [girls can]⟩
Mother:	Girls can or can't, did you say? ⟨Question Stereotype⟩
Child:	Can. ⟨Affirm Stereotype⟩
Mother:	So boys and girls can. ⟨Negate Stereotype [boys can]⟩ ⟨Affirm Stereotype [girls can]⟩

Speakers' sensitivity to context is important, as it suggests that the input children hear may be strongly influenced by the materials provided. Interestingly, however, the differences are not always in the direction one might predict, based on the content provided on the page. What we find most notable about this constellation of results is that they seem to indicate two seemingly contradictory correlates of stereotype-inconsistent models going on simultaneously: a greater focus on gender categories (generics, gender-ostensive labeling, gender contrasts) *and* more talk of gender-egalitarianism (counter-stereotyping, gender equality statements). This suggests that variation in speech across contexts cannot be characterized along a single dimension of degree of gender-typing. Rather, there seemed to be differences in how focused a speaker was on gender (or not), with some contexts associated with more talk about gender—both stereotyped and non-stereotyped—and others associated with less such talk. This finding fits well with the explicit/implicit distinction made at the beginning of the General Discussion. Even when a mother attempts to be gender-egalitarian in her explicit statements about gender stereotypes, she may implicitly emphasize and encourage a focus on gender as a basis for categorizing the social world.

These findings are reminiscent of an early argument by Bem (1983). She suggested that even gender-egalitarian input still provides a powerful focus on gender. In attempting to neutralize gender or take it out of the equation, this strategy can inadvertently create an even greater focus on gender. Likewise, DeLoache, Cassidy, and Carpenter (1987) make the point that creating gender-neutral picture books will not eliminate sexist input to children, because book-reading is mediated by people who read the books (parents, teachers, older siblings). For example, even when gender-neutral characters are presented, adults tend to interpret them as male. Our data fully support the hypothesis that gender-egalitarian input nonetheless emphasizes gender, with both parental and child speech. How to reduce the child's focus on gender, in the face of such paradoxical highlighting of gender, is unclear. However, it may be that the goal of gender-egalitarian parenting is not to make gender a less salient dimension, but to make it just one of many ways of interpreting incoming information.

Weisner and Wilson-Mitchell (1990), who studied gender-role socialization in five distinct types of nonconventional families, including those who were firmly committed to promoting gender-egalitarian beliefs in their children, found that the non-gender-typed children in their sample were *multischematic* rather than *aschematic* with respect to gender. That is, the non-gender-typed children were "simultaneously aware of and selectively practiced more than one way to classify information by gender" (p. 1930). They concluded that children whose parents promote gender-egalitarian beliefs may differ from children exposed to more traditional beliefs in that they may have "a lower threshold for spontaneously using different kinds of gender-typing models, rather than replacing one model with another" (p. 1930). This argument follows from Bem's (1985) discussion of individual differences in gender typing, in which she views gender-typed individuals as differing from others "not in their *ability* to organize information on the basis of gender but in their *threshold* for doing so spontaneously" (p. 197).

CHILDREN'S EARLY GENDER BELIEFS

One goal of this project was to examine changes with age in children's talk about gender. A number of studies have shown that gender stereotyping emerges during the preschool years (between 2 and 4 years of age), peaks at about 5–7 years of age, and then becomes more flexible in middle childhood (see Martin, Ruble, & Szkrybalo, 2002, for a review). However, more mixed developmental patterns have been seen with children's gender-related preferences and behaviors (Ruble & Martin, 1998). The current data allow an examination of these issues by presenting evidence from children's gender-related talk. One advantage of examining children's talk is that it is relatively unconstrained (e.g., children could choose to focus on gender categories, gendered individuals, or dimensions other than gender). By studying three distinct age groups over this rapidly changing period, we can examine these developmental issues.

In our data, the most notable age-related changes take place between 2 and 4 years of age. When we examined how often children affirm or negate gender stereotypes, children showed little awareness of the gender stereotypes tested at age 2, but consistently stereotyped beliefs by 4 years of age. Correspondingly, we found sharp increases between 2 and 4 in the frequency of generics, as well as higher rates of gender contrasts and gender equality statements. By 4 years of age, children are expressive and often quite firm in their attention to and beliefs about gender. In contrast, the changes taking place between 4 and 6 years of age are more modest and subtle. We illustrate these changes with a comparison of three different excerpts, from children at ages 2, 4, and 6, respectively.

First is a rather typical exchange with a 2-year-old (girl, age 2.7 years), where the focus is on specific individuals, and less clearly on gender. Note the child's reference to particular people (you, Daddy, John), and no reference to gender per se. (Person scope and stereotype affirmations, negations, and questions are indicated in pointed brackets.)

Mother:	"Who can play with toy trucks?"
Mother:	Hm?
Child:	Um, you. ⟨Individual⟩ ⟨Negate Stereotype⟩
Mother:	I can. ⟨Individual⟩ ⟨Negate Stereotype⟩
Mother:	Yes, I like to play with trucks. ⟨Individual⟩ ⟨Negate Stereotype⟩
Mother:	Who else can play with trucks? ⟨Other Scope⟩ ⟨Question Stereotype⟩

Mother:	Hm?
Child:	Um, you. ⟨Individual⟩ ⟨Negate Stereotype⟩
Mother:	Yeah, well who else? ⟨Other Scope⟩ ⟨Question Stereotype⟩
Child:	Maybe Daddy. ⟨Individual⟩ ⟨Affirm Stereotype⟩
Mother:	Daddy, yeah. ⟨Individual⟩ ⟨Affirm Stereotype⟩
Child:	Maybe John.[12] ⟨Individual⟩ ⟨Affirm Stereotype⟩
Mother:	Yeah.
Child:	Maybe Daddy. ⟨Individual⟩ ⟨Affirm Stereotype⟩
Mother:	Yeah.

Contrast this with the following conversation between a mother and her 4.3-year-old son. Note the overt stereotyping ("only boys"), gender-based generics, and explicit mention of gender when labeling ("sail-man"). (Person scope and stereotype affirmations, negations, and questions are indicated in pointed brackets.)

Mother:	Who's driving the boat? ⟨Individual⟩ ⟨Question Stereotype⟩
Child:	A sail-man. ⟨Individual⟩ ⟨Affirm Stereotype⟩
Mother:	A sail-man. ⟨Individual⟩ ⟨Affirm Stereotype⟩
Mother:	Yup, a sailor. ... ⟨Individual⟩ ⟨Affirm Stereotype⟩
Mother:	"Who can be a sailor?"
Mother:	Boys and girls? ⟨Generic⟩ ⟨Question Stereotype⟩
Child:	Boys. ⟨Generic⟩ ⟨Affirm Stereotype⟩
Mother:	Boys, okay. ⟨Generic⟩ ⟨Affirm Stereotype⟩
Child:	Only boys. ⟨Generic⟩ ⟨Affirm Stereotype⟩
Mother:	Only boys. ⟨Generic⟩ ⟨Affirm Stereotype⟩

Finally, in the following exchange between a mother and her child (a boy aged 6.3 years), the child endorses a gender stereotype and makes reference to generic kinds, as did the 4-year-old. Additionally, the 6-year-old implies an essential basis to the gender difference, with speculations about gender-linked "skills." Coding of person scope, stereotype affirmations, negations, and questions, and gender contrasts are indicated in pointed brackets:

Mother:	"Who can knit a sweater?"
Child:	Girls. ⟨Generic⟩ ⟨Affirm Stereotype⟩
Child:	But not boys. ⟨Generic⟩ ⟨Affirm Stereotype⟩ ⟨Gender Contrast⟩
Mother:	Now why's that?
Child:	Boys don't have those, special skills. ⟨Generic⟩ ⟨Affirm Stereotype⟩
Mother:	Okay.

Child: They have wood chopping skills or racing skills. ⟨Generic⟩
                ⟨Affirm Stereotype⟩

At the oldest age, we sometimes see a grudging acceptance of the possibility of counter-stereotypical activities, as in the following exchange between a mother and her son, age 6.09 years. Stereotype affirmations, negations, and questions are presented in pointed brackets:

Mother: Does Cynthia[13] ever play with trucks? ⟨Question Stereotype⟩
Child: Sometimes. ⟨Negate Stereotype⟩
Child: Girl trucks.
Mother: What are girl trucks?
Child: Pink ones.
Mother: Does Cynthia have pink trucks? ⟨Question Stereotype⟩
Child: Yeah. ⟨Negate Stereotype⟩
Mother: Really?
Child: [nods "yes"]
Child: Well she has pink cars but not pink trucks. ⟨Affirm Stereotype⟩
Mother: So she, drives, the cars while you and Brian[14] drive the trucks?
                ⟨Question Stereotype⟩
Child: Yup. ⟨Affirm Stereotype⟩ ⟨Negate Stereotype⟩

To summarize, these excerpts illustrate the increase with age in children's attention to generics (especially between 2 and 4 years), as well as the increasing acknowledgment of counter-stereotypical examples (especially at age 6). It is interesting that the major developmental shifts take place *before* the age of 4. These findings suggest that gender constancy (at least as traditionally measured) is not required for the emergence of well-articulated gender categories. Instead, this finding supports other research arguing that important understandings emerge in the early preschool years (Martin, Ruble, & Szkrybalo, 2002).

One question raised by the developmental data is why the most conspicuous changes are taking place between 2 and 4 years of age. Note that the developmental patterns we have obtained cannot be attributed to age-related changes in the amount of talk, because all analyses controlled for the number of utterances produced by each speaker. Rather, there are changes in the focus and content of the talk that is produced. Whereas 2-year-olds tend to be focused on *individuals* (including those depicted in the book, or others outside the book context), 4- and 6-year-olds are more focused on generic *kinds*. This shift is consistent with other language analyses finding a sharp increase between 2 and 4 years of age in the frequency of generics overall (not just those referring to gender; Gelman, 2003). The increased attention to kinds therefore does not seem to be specific to gender, but may

105

instead reflect a greater ease with which children can consider abstract categories of people.

Another possibility to consider is whether the changes reflect differences in how *mothers* speak to 2- vs. 4- or 6-year-olds. After all, we did find many of the same increases with age (in generics, gender contrasts, and gender equality statements) in maternal talk as with child talk. However, data from the dyadic analyses of generics suggest that the increases in production of generics between 2 and 4 years of age originate primarily in the children, not the mothers. The following example, between a mother and her son age 4.99, shows that even when the mother attempts to introduce counter-stereotype information, the child persists in negating it. Stereotype affirmations, negations, and questions are presented in pointed brackets:

Mother:	"Who can be a ballet dancer?"
Child:	I don't know. ⟨Question Stereotype⟩
Child:	Why is that a boy? [Child is referring to picture in book, which shows a man ballet dancer.]
Mother:	Well, can a boy be a ballet dancer? ⟨Question Stereotype⟩
Child:	No. ⟨Affirm Stereotype⟩
Mother:	Why not?
Child:	[sighs]
Mother:	I've seen boy ballet dancers. ⟨Negate Stereotype⟩
Child:	I don't think so. ⟨Affirm Stereotype⟩

A further question we may ask is: what understandings of gender can we see at the youngest age? In this study, the most sensitive indices of 2-year-old children's knowledge of gender and gender stereotypes emerged from their labeling. Two-year-olds performed quite well on the gender-labeling task they received after the book-reading session. They also were highly accurate in how they referred to pictures during the book-reading session: nearly 80% of children's references to people in the picture books conveyed the appropriate gender (with either a noun, pronoun, or proper name). Finally, children's references to people in the picture book turned out to be a sensitive index of their knowledge of gender stereotypes, as well. Two-year-olds made significantly more naming errors when discussing counter-stereotypic pictures (e.g., woman race-car driver) than stereotypic pictures (e.g., woman feeding a baby), thereby indicating an association between stereotypic activities and gender. In contrast to the sensitivity of their labels, in other respects 2-year-olds provided little evidence of gender stereotyping. For example, they rarely referred to generic categories of gender, rarely contrasted male vs. female, and were no more likely to affirm gender stereotypes than to negate gender stereotypes. The patterns of performance here are consistent with prior research demonstrating that gender stereotypes are initially more flexible in very young preschool children, and become less flexible until middle elementary-school age, when flexibility increases (a U-shaped pattern; Katz & Ksansnak, 1994; Signorella, Bigler, & Liben, 1993). Altogether, our data confirm that gender stereotyping is ongoing in development, and they illustrate the need for sensitive measures of young children's knowledge.

A final developmental issue that we wish to highlight is that, with increasing age, children become *simultaneously* more focused on gender categories and gender stereotypes *and* more gender-egalitarian. Thus, at the same time that we see striking increases with age in generics and gender contrasts, we also see much higher frequency of explicit statements regarding gender equality. This set of findings again supports the conclusion that knowledge and beliefs cannot be characterized along a single dimension of gender-stereotyping. Although logically it may seem contradictory for stereotyping and egalitarianism to increase simultaneously, from a developmental perspective these can be seen as two aspects of an increasingly complex, increasingly detailed gender concept. Killen, Pisacane, Lee-Kim, and Artila-Rey (2001) similarly report that preschool children (4-1/2 and 5-1/2 years of age) make use of two distinct types of knowledge when reasoning about who to include or exclude in a group: moral knowledge (based on judgments of fairness) and social–conventional knowledge (based on gender stereotypes). For example, when asked to select either a boy or a girl to join a group of girls playing with dolls, 4-year-olds typically selected a girl, but when asked if it was all right or not all right to exclude a boy, 87% judged that it would be morally wrong (e.g., "it wouldn't be fair"). It appears that children can consider both the moral and the social-conventional frameworks, and that different contexts or probes elicit different ways of reasoning about gender stereotypes and gender-relevant behavior.

LINKS BETWEEN MATERNAL TALK AND CHILD TALK

Mother–Child Similarities

Despite some differences between mother and child talk (most notably, much higher endorsement of gender stereotypes among children than among mothers), there was also remarkably high consistency between mothers and children. Mothers and children showed similar patterns of age-related increases: in generics, contrasts, and egalitarian statements. Mothers and children also showed similar effects of the various manipulations that were examined (such as page consistency or sex-of-referent). Finally, individual differences in four of the six measures showed significant positive correlations between mothers and children: generics, gender-ostensive labeling, gender contrasts, and gender equality statements. A fifth measure (negating gender stereotypes) showed a trend in the expected direction.

Overall, then, mothers and children are quite similar in what they say. The reason for these commonalities is not well understood. One prime question is whether the similarities are situation-specific or reflect more enduring individual differences. Past work has shown that gender effects in parents' speech can be moderated by the context (e.g., with greater gender effects during unstructured activities; Leaper et al., 1998). In the case of the high mother–child correlations obtained here, context may be important in that both mother and child were discussing the same picture book. Mothers and children may sound alike because the data came from conversations in which mothers and children were talking to one another, and thus accommodating to each other. Perhaps any two people in a conversation start to reflect one another's speech styles. Just as the topic of conversation is typically shared across both speakers, perhaps too the style of conversation (e.g., frequency of generics) is also shared across both speakers. Similarly, Leaper (2002) cautions that parent–child correlations may also reflect child effects on parents (not simply parent effects on children), with the behavior of particular children evoking certain sorts of responses on the part of parents (see also Scarr & McCartney, 1983).

On the other hand, there may be more stable individual differences that mothers and children share. Children who hear many generics from their mothers may more readily talk about generic *categories* of gender, as opposed to gendered individuals. This relationship, if verified, would then raise the question of whether distinctive patterns of talk correspond to distinctive patterns of thought. For example, do children who hear many gender-based generics then more readily construe individuals in terms of their gender category, perhaps even overriding individual variation? The nature of the underlying causal mechanisms and consequences for thought are questions that await future research.

Maternal Responses to Child Stereotyping

Another aspect of parental input involved mothers' responses to child stereotyping. In our sample, maternal responses to children's stereotypes were surprisingly mild. Mothers rarely negated children's gender stereotypes, and in fact primarily affirmed what children said. In a sense, then, mothers were complicit with children's stereotyping statements. The following example of a conversation between a mother and her daughter, 6.49 years of age, illustrates this tacit acceptance of gender stereotyping. (Child's stereotype affirmations and maternal responses are indicated in pointed brackets.)

Child:	"Who can be a balle, ballet dancer?"
Child:	Girls. ⟨Affirm Stereotype⟩
Mother:	Are you a ballet dancer? ⟨Response: Question-Expand (Same Gender)⟩
Child:	Yes. ⟨Affirm Stereotype⟩
Mother:	What about Paul?[15] ⟨Question-Expand (New Gender)⟩
Mother:	Could he be one?
Child:	No! [shakes head 'no'] ⟨Affirm Stereotype⟩
Mother:	No? ⟨Question-Repeat⟩
Child:	Boys don't ever be, ballet dancers. ⟨Affirm Stereotype⟩

[The dyad then moved on to the next page in the book. Therefore, the mother's response was coded as ⟨Other⟩.]

However, when mothers did provide a negative response, it was much more often in response to children's negative-valence statements than to their positive-valence statements. We therefore found a bias in maternal responses to child stereotyping: positive-valence stereotypes (e.g., "A grown-up man" [can take out the trash]) were treated as innocuous, whereas negative-valence stereotypes (e.g., "Um-um ⟨no⟩, no, boys can't" [play with dolls]) were treated as considerably more serious. It would be interesting to know if children's interpretation of positive- vs. negative-valence stereotypes are also asymmetric. Are negative-valence statements understood by children as more informative about gender stereotypes than positive-valence statements? For example, if a child learns that Jimmy can do X, and that Nathan can't do Y, which property is more likely to generalize to other boys—the positive conclusion (boys can do X) or the negative conclusion (boys can't do Y)? Similar questions arise for generics (e.g., is a child more likely to draw conclusions about what girls can or cannot do after hearing a positive generic about boys, or after hearing a negative generic about boys?). It may be that mothers' responses reflect a true difference between positive- and negative-valence information in what they tell children about stereotypes. Or it may be that mothers are overly sanguine about positive stereotypes, in that they are interpreted in powerful ways by children but viewed as relatively innocuous by mothers.

Maternal Language Effects?

An important open question that this study does not address is how children *use* the information that parents are providing. Do the patterns that we have uncovered have measurable effects on children's gender stereotyping and gender concepts, or are they unrelated to children's gender concept development? If a child hears many generics about gender, for example, does this encourage the child to conceptualize gender categories as more coherent or worthy of generalizations? These questions are deeply tied to the larger theoretical debate concerning the role of parents in socializing gender concepts in children (e.g., Maccoby, 1998). The constructivist model of gender concept acquisition, sketched out in Chapter 1, would suggest that gender concepts are neither innately given nor an exact copy of the information children receive from others. Instead, children create gender concepts on the basis of information supplied in the input. The current findings are consistent with this model. We found that children are not provided with much in the way of *direct* or *explicit* gender stereotyping. Thus, gender essentialism is unlikely to be a belief system that children passively absorb from messages provided by mothers in the input. However, the information children receive from mothers is rich with indirect cues that, when interpreted coherently, suggest the possibility of gender essentialism. That is, the indirect cues children hear in the input could be fodder for children's construction of essentialist beliefs.

At this point we have no direct evidence regarding the effects of maternal speech on children's gender essentialism. Nonetheless, we can speculate about such effects on the basis of past research. Past work has found that when children learn new properties about animal species that are phrased in generic noun phrases (e.g., "Bears have three layers of fur"), they generalize such properties more broadly than when such properties are attributed to only "some" members of a category ("Some bears have three layers of fur"). A similar effect may take place with social categories, including gender. That is, statements regarding "girls" as a group or "boys" as a group may be assumed to generalize broadly to instances of the category as a whole. Furthermore, Bigler (1995) has found that when teachers make functional use of gender, elementary-school children (6–11 years of age) engage in more of an own-sex bias in attitudes. (See also Bigler, Jones, & Lobliner, 1997, for similar findings when teachers make functional use of minimal groups, e.g., children wearing blue vs. yellow shirts.) Of particular interest here is the fact that one of the manipulations in Bigler's study includes use of reference to gender groupings, pulling together all members of a gendered group within the classroom (e.g., "*All the boys* should be sitting down," "*All the girls* put their bubble-makers in the air," "Amber, you can come up for *the girls*," "Jack, be a good helper for *the boys*"; emphases added). These references are not generic per se, but are similar to generics in implying commonalities among members of a group and highlighting salience of the group per se. Put somewhat differently, highlighting gender categories appears to increase children's gender stereotyping, and generics provide a means of highlighting gender.

In the introduction, we noted that some previous authors have concluded that parents play a minimal role during gender socialization (e.g.,

Lytton & Romney, 1991; Maccoby, 2002; but see Tenenbaum & Leaper, 2002, for a meta-analysis showing small, positive correlations between parental gender attitudes and children's gender attitudes). The current data suggest one possible explanation for this result: parents may not typically communicate their beliefs explicitly. Instead, children may infer from their parents' *implicit* essentialist language that their parents endorse gender-stereotyped responses, and adopt these beliefs. Although children are active learners and parents are unlikely to shape children's beliefs directly, mothers' linguistic input does seem to convey subtle messages about gender from which children may construct their own essentialist beliefs.

IMPLICATIONS FOR THE STUDY OF LANGUAGE AND GENDER

The research reported in this monograph is part of a larger tradition that examines how language affects gender concepts. Here we briefly review that work with the goal of clarifying how the present findings complement the literature. Henley (1989) notes that there are three forms of sex imbalance in language: (1) language can be used to deprecate women (e.g., with more words available to refer to sexually promiscuous women than sexually promiscuous men); (2) language can be used to ignore women (e.g., male nouns or pronouns used to refer to either males or females, as in "Every person should get out *his* notebook"); and (3) language can be used to express gender stereotypes, especially stereotypes of women (e.g., with phrases such as "lady doctor" or "male stewardess," or with titles that emphasize the marital status of women more than men, with Miss/Mrs. vs. Mr.). (See also Crawford, 2001, for a very similar analysis, and Graddol & Swann, 1989, for many insightful examples of sex imbalances in language.)

The majority of prior research on language and gender has focused on the use of male words (e.g., "he," "man") to refer to females as well as males—the so-called "generic" uses. At this point we pause to note that the terminology here is potentially confusing. We have used the word "generic" throughout the monograph to refer to noun phrases that express general categories rather than specific individuals—phrases such as "boys," "women," or "little kids." In contrast, "generic" in the present context refers to a use of the male noun or pronoun to refer to an indefinite person regardless of gender. In order to differentiate the two uses, we will use the phrase "generic *he*" to refer to an ungendered meaning for a male word, and we will use "generic" or "generic noun phrase" to refer to nouns or pronouns that make general reference.

The question of greatest interest regarding the generic *he* is how it is interpreted by speakers, either adults or children. In particular, when a gender-neutral meaning is intended, is a gender-neutral meaning conveyed, or do people interpret generic *he* as male-referring? A variety of studies show that generic *he* is typically interpreted as referring to a male referent rather than being gender-neutral (Conkright, Flannagan, & Dykes, 2000; Gastil, 1990; Henley, 1989; Switzer, 1990), for children as well as adults (Hyde, 1984). Relatedly, in a book-reading task with mothers and their young children (18 months to 3 years of age), mothers are strongly biased toward referring to gender-neutral animal characters as male (DeLoache, Cassidy, & Carpenter, 1987). These findings illustrate the perhaps-unintended sexism implicit in language use.

The work reported in this monograph focuses on a different function of language: use of language to express gender stereotypes. However, although our focus is relatively new in terms of which expressions we examine and how they function, we find a common theme with past work: language may be particularly powerful when it expresses gender essentialism *indirectly.* DeLoache et al. (1987, pp. 164–165) propose:

> Much of the information that parents transmit to their young children is conveyed not only indirectly, but unintentionally as well. ... [A]dults unwittingly behave differently to boys and girls, and in the process communicate gender-stereotyped information to them.

Similarly, Henley (1989), citing MacKay (1980), suggests that generic *he* is so potent because it has the properties of "highly effective propaganda techniques," including frequency, covertness, early age of acquisition, indirectness, and association with high-prestige. These same "propaganda techniques" apply to the use of generics in the speech of mothers and their young children: general categories of gender (with generics), gender-ostensive labeling, and gender contrasts. All of these forms occur relatively frequently, covertly, and indirectly, and are acquired at an early age. They may also be associated with high prestige, to the extent that parents have prestige in the eyes of their children. Perhaps such indirect uses of language have more significant consequences than direct expression of gender stereotypes.

GENERALIZABILITY OF THESE DATA

How far can we generalize the current findings to other contexts, settings, or speakers? The participants were given minimal instructions or directions, so their talk was relatively spontaneous and unstructured. However, several aspects of the situation may have influenced the nature of the talk, and it would be important in the future to vary these conditions.

Certainly, the fact that the books were clearly about gendered activities undoubtedly prompted a higher focus on gender than would otherwise be seen. It would be interesting, for example, to examine gender-related talk in the CHILDES transcripts (MacWhinney & Snow, 1990), to examine which of these implicit and explicit strategies are found in ordinary conversations that don't involve a gendered prompt. When the context is more open-ended, we also might find more striking individual differences in how frequently gender even comes up as a topic of conversation.

More specifically with these books, as already mentioned, gender-atypical pages were talked about differently than gender-typical pages. On gender-atypical pages, speakers provided more counter-stereotyping messages and more gender-egalitarian messages, as well as more gender-ostensive labeling and gender contrasts. It is possible that ordinary picture books and settings are more likely to conform to gender stereotypes than to contradict them, thereby being associated with more gender-stereotyping messages overall than were found here. In other words, if we were to analyze just the gender-typical pages, we might find a more representative picture of the kinds of maternal input that children hear. Recall that when looking just at gender-consistent pages (e.g., man chopping wood, girl playing with doll), both mothers and children affirmed gender stereotypes more than negated them.

The text of the picture books asked "Who *can*…?" (emphasis added), thereby providing a conservative test of gender-essentialist language. Both children and adults are more accepting of the possibility that males *can* engage in traditionally female activities, or that females *can* engage in traditionally male activities, even if they strongly believe that such activities *should* not take place (Levy, Taylor, & Gelman, 1995). It would be interesting to contrast the current findings with a comparable picture book in which the text asks, "Who *should* …?" Here we suspect that we would obtain even stronger evidence of gender-stereotyped messages, certainly from children and perhaps also from mothers.

Aside from particulars regarding the book-reading context, we do not know how social desirability factors may have influenced mothers' speech. Mothers may have been on "good" behavior, and especially likely to talk in non-sexist or non-stereotyped fashion. If this was so, our data would underestimate the occurrence of gendered speech that children hear. Nonetheless, it is interesting that despite any such pressures to play down sexist talk, gendered generics were still quite frequent. Conversely, perhaps a desire to be polite and well-behaved, or a desire to elicit talk from the child, kept parents from disagreeing more vociferously with their children. Directly disagreeing with the child was rare. These issues again could be fruitfully addressed with an examination of natural language transcripts from more open-ended conversational topics.

Finally, we cannot take these conversations as fully representative of the sorts of talk that children hear, given tremendous variation in the importance and emphasis placed on gender, across individuals and across cultural contexts. The present study was conducted in a highly-educated, middle-class university town. Presumably gender attitudes are relatively more liberal in this sample. Mothers in a more traditional community might provide more explicit pronouncements about gender. Also, we examined only mothers. Past work has found that mothers and fathers react differently to their children's gender-stereotyped behaviors, with fathers displaying fewer positive reactions (Fagot & Hagan, 1991). Fathers' differential treatment of sons vs. daughters emerges by 12 months of age (Snow, Jacklin, & Maccoby, 1983). Moreover, fathers appear to differentiate between boys and girls more than do mothers (Siegal, 1987). See Leaper et al. (1998) for a review of numerous other ways in which fathers talk differently to their children than mothers. It would be interesting to replicate the present study with fathers, to obtain a broader sense of the kinds of input that children are receiving. Fathers may express gender-stereotyped attitudes more directly, for example. More generally, it would be interesting to extend this study to contexts, cultures, and subcultures that more readily support gender stereotypes, and see how the parent–child conversations differ correspondingly. Furthermore, teachers, siblings, peers, schools, and the media all are potentially powerful sources of information to young children and would be an important supplement to the current focus on mothers.

CONCLUSIONS

In the development of gender stereotyping and gender concepts, what is the role of language relative to other sorts of input? The field of cognitive development has demonstrated children's early and keen sensitivity to subtleties of language, and their effects on categorization (Bloom, 2000; Bowerman & Levinson, 2001; Choi & Bowerman, 1991; Gentner & Goldin-Meadow, 2003; Gopnik, Choi, & Baumberger, 1996; Hall & Waxman, 1993; Imai & Gentner, 1997; Waxman, 1999). Moreover, in the field of linguistic anthropology, language is recognized as a powerful socializing influence (Ochs & Schieffelin, 1984). Language is one of the most ubiquitous, early-acquired, and powerful forms of cultural transmission available to our species. From this perspective, it would be surprising if the language that parents use did not have an effect. Although the present study has not examined the *effects* of language on children's gender concepts, it provides a critical first step: a detailed characterization of what information the language provides (see also Callanan, 1990; Gelman et al., 1998, for models).

How revealing is language as a window onto children's gender concepts? In our data, what participants *said* (in the picture-book task) correlated moderately well with their responses on the gender-typing and gender-constancy measures. This finding suggests that natural language conversations do provide a sensitive means of tapping into beliefs that are gauged by more traditional survey methods. Yet researchers have been rightly cautious about interpreting what children say as a direct reflection of their beliefs (e.g., Karmiloff-Smith, 1977). The field of cognitive development has moved increasingly toward more subtle measures of children's concepts (see, for example, the entire subfield of infant cognition).

Nonetheless, children's talk provides potentially important insights onto children's beliefs, as well as advantages not found in other methods. Shatz (1994) provides a powerful case study using natural language as a basis for gleaning insights about cognitive, linguistic, and social developments over the toddler years. Likewise, we have seen at least three advantages of natural language analyses in the present study: (1) Because natural language is a common and familiar form of expression for young children, it provides a sensitive index of what young children know, at an age where they may be more limited on experimental tasks. (2) Conversations are open-ended in content and therefore enable us to gauge children's interest in a topic (for example, how often they discuss gendered vs. non-gendered categories). (3) The interactive nature of conversation allows us to study the contexts in which children express different sorts of beliefs. In the present study, the patterns in children's natural language revealed unexpected insights into the distinction between category and individual in children's gender concepts (see also Biernat, 1991). We therefore conclude that language is a rich source of information to researchers, and potentially to young children as well.

NOTES

11. Pseudonym.
12. Pseudonym.
13. Pseudonym.
14. Pseudonym.
15. Pseudonym.

GENDER LABELING TASK (2-YEAR-OLDS ONLY)

[child sees picture of boy and girl]
Which one is named Michael?
Is Michael a boy or a girl?
Which one is named Emily?
Is Emily a boy or a girl?
Who said, "My name is Michael"? Show me the one who said that.
Who said, "My name is Emily"? Show me the one who said that.
Who said, "I'm a boy"? Show me the one who said that.
Who said, "I'm a girl"? Show me the one who said that.

[child sees picture of man and woman]
Which one is named John?
Is John a man or a woman?
Which one is named Katie?
Is Katie a man or a woman?
Who said, "My name is John"? Show me the one who said that.
Who said, "My name is Katie"? Show me the one who said that.
Who said, "I'm a man"? Show me the one who said that.
Who said, "I'm a woman"? Show me the one who said that.

APPENDIX B
ITEMS IN GENDER-STEREOTYPE FLEXIBILITY TASK
(4- AND 6-YEAR-OLDS ONLY)

Stereotypically Male Items

help fix a car (1.8)
play with a train set* (2.6)
help build with tools (2.0)
play basketball (2.4)
be a plumber [fix a toilet] (2.0)

play baseball* (2.6)
be a garbage collector [pick up trash] (1.8)
mow the lawn [cut grass]* (2.6)

Stereotypically Female Items

play with a tea set* (6.4)
play jump rope (5.4)
help iron clothes (6.0)
help cook dinner (5.4)
be a babysitter (5.8)
be a librarian [work with books] (6.1)
bake a pie* (5.6)
go grocery shopping [shop for food] (5.4)

Gender-Neutral Items

watch TV
help wash the dishes
play tennis
be a musician [make music]

Note: Mean ratings appear in parentheses. The wording for 2-year-olds appears in brackets, when different from that for 4- and 6-year-olds. Most ratings are from the COAT (Liben & Bigler, 2002), a 7-point scale where 1 = for males only and 7 = for females only. Those indicated with an asterisk were from our pre-test measure with adults, a 5-point scale where 1 = only boys/men; 5 = only girls/women. In order to make the two scales comparable, the pre-test scores were converted to a 7-point scale in this table.

APPENDIX C
CHILD GENDER CONSTANCY MEASURE (NON-SELF)
(4- AND 6-YEAR-OLDS ONLY)

Khwan (Girl)

[Experimenter labels picture of baby as a "girl" named "Khwan".]
Can you point to Khwan?
Is Khwan a boy or a girl?
[If the answer is "girl," ask:] Is Khwan a boy?
What does Khwan look like, a boy or a girl?

What is Khwan really, a boy or a girl?

What makes Khwan really a boy/girl?

[following change of appearance, so that Khwan is wearing boy clothes]:

    What does Khwan look like, a boy or a girl?

    What is Khwan really, a boy or a girl?

    What makes Khwan really a boy/girl?

Gaw (Boy)

[Experimenter labels picture of baby as a "boy" named "Gaw".]

Can you point to Gaw?

Is Gaw a boy or a girl?

[If the answer is "boy," ask:] Is Gaw a girl?

What does Gaw look like, a boy or a girl?

What is Gaw really, a boy or a girl?

What makes Gaw really a boy/girl?

[following change of appearance, so that Gaw is wearing girl clothes]:

    What does Gaw look like, a boy or a girl?

    What is Gaw really, a boy or a girl?

    What makes Gaw really a boy/girl?

APPENDIX D
MATERNAL GENDER-TYPING TASKS

What I want to be: OAT-PM (short version) *plus* garbage collector, plumber, librarian.

What I do in my free time: OAT-PM (short version) *plus* play with model trainset, bake a pie, play baseball, fix a car, mow the lawn, jump rope, use a teaset, play basketball.

What I am like: OAT-PM (short version)

Who should do these jobs: OAT-AM (short) *plus* babysitter, garbage collector.

Who should do these activities: OAT-AM (short) *plus* model trainset, mow lawn, iron clothes, bake pie, play baseball, jump rope, cook dinner, use a teaset, and play basketball.

Who should be this way: OAT-AM (short)

Note: OAT-PM and OAT-AM can be found in Liben and Bigler (2002).

REFERENCES

Au, T. K., & Laframboise, D. E. (1990). Acquiring color names via linguistic contrast: The influence of contrasting terms. *Child Development*, **61**, 1808–1823.

Bakeman, R., & Gottman, J. M. (1997). *Observing interaction: An introduction to sequential analysis* (2nd ed.). New York: Cambridge University Press.

Baldwin, D. A., Markman, E. M., & Melartin, R. L. (1993). Infants' ability to draw inferences about nonobvious object properties: Evidence from exploratory play. *Cognitive Development*, **64**, 711–728.

Bartsch, K., & Wellman, H. M. (1995). *Children talk about the mind*. New York: Oxford University Press.

Bauer, P. J., & Coyne, M. J. (1997). When the name says it all: Preschoolers' recognition and use of the gendered nature of common proper names. *Social Development*, **6**, 271–291.

Bem, S. L. (1983). Gender schema theory and its implications for child development: Raising gender-aschematic children in a gender-schematic society. *Signs*, **8**, 598–616.

Bem, S. L. (1985). Androgyny and gender schema theory: A conceptual and empirical integration. In T. B. Sonderegger (Ed.), *Nebraska symposium on motivation: Psychology of gender* (Vol. 32, pp. 179–222). Lincoln: University of Nebraska Press.

Bem, S. (1989). Genital knowledge and gender constancy in preschool children. *Child Development*, **60**, 620–649.

Bem, S. L. (1995). Dismantling gender polarization and compulsory heterosexuality: Should we turn the volume up or down? *Journal of Sex Research*, **32**, 329–334.

Biernat, M. (1991). Gender stereotypes and the relationship between masculinity and femininity: A developmental analysis. *Journal of Personality and Social Psychology*, **61**, 351–365.

Bigler, R. S. (1995). The role of classification skill in moderating environmental influences on children's gender stereotyping: A study of the functional use of gender in the classroom. *Child Development*, **66**, 1072–1082.

Bigler, R. S. (1997). Conceptual and methodological issues in the measurement of children's sex typing. *Psychology of Women Quarterly*, **21**, 53–69.

Bigler, R. S. (1999). Psychological interventions designed to counter sexism in children: Empirical limitations and theoretical foundations. In W. B. Swann, J. H. Langlois & L. A. Gilbert (Eds.), *Sexism and stereotypes in modern society: The gender science of Janet Taylor Spence* (pp. 129–151). Washington, DC: American Psychological Association.

Bigler, R. S., Jones, L. C., & Lobliner, D. B. (1997). Social categorization and the formation of intergroup attitudes in children. *Child Development*, **68**, 530–543.

Bigler, R. S., & Liben, L. S. (1990). The role of attitudes and interventions in gender-schematic processing. *Child Development*, **61**, 1440–1452.

Bigler, R. S., & Liben, L. S. (1992). Cognitive mechanisms in children's gender stereotyping: Theoretical and educational implications of a cognitive-based intervention. *Child Development*, **63**, 1351–1363.

Bjorklund, D. F. (2000). *Children's thinking: Developmental function and individual differences* (3rd ed.). Belmont, CA: Wadsworth/Thomson Learning.

Blair, I. V., & Banaji, M. R. (1996). Automatic and controlled processes in stereotype priming. *Journal of Personality and Social Psychology, 70*, 1142–1163.

Bloom, P. (2000). *How children learn the meanings of words.* Cambridge, MA: MIT Press.

Bohan, J. S. (1993). Regarding gender: Essentialism, constructionism, and feminist psychology. *Psychology of Women Quarterly, 17*, 5–21.

Bowerman, M., & Levinson, S. C. (Eds.) (2001). *Language acquisition and conceptual development.* New York: Cambridge University Press.

Bradbard, M. R., & Endsley, R. C. (1983). The effects of sex-typed labeling on preschool children's information-seeking and retention. *Sex Roles, 9*, 247–260.

Bradbard, M. R., Martin, C. L., Endsley, R. C., & Halverson, C. F. (1986). The influence of sex stereotypes on children's exploration and memory: A competence versus performance distinction. *Developmental Psychology, 22*, 481–486.

Bussey, K., & Bandura, A. (1999). Social cognitive theory of gender development and differentiation. *Psychological Review, 106*, 676–713.

Bussey, K., & Perry, D. G. (1982). Same-sex imitation: The avoidance of cross-sex models or the acceptance of same-sex models? *Sex Roles, 8*, 773–784.

Callanan, M. A. (1985). How parents label objects for young children: The role of input in the acquisition of category hierarchies. *Child Development, 56*, 508–523.

Callanan, M. A. (1990). Parents' descriptions of objects: Potential data for children's inferences about category principles. *Cognitive Development, 5*, 101–122.

Calvert, S. L., & Huston, A. C. (1987). Television and children's gender schemata. In L. S. Liben & M. L. Signorella (Eds.), *New directions for child development: Vol. 38. Children's gender schemata* (pp. 75–88). San Francisco: Jossey-Bass.

Carlson, G. N. & Pelletier, F. J. (Eds.) (1995). *The generic book.* Chicago: University of Chicago Press.

Choi, S., & Bowerman, M. (1991). Learning to express motion events in English and Korean: The influence of language-specific lexicalization patterns. *Cognition, 41*, 83–121.

Clark, E. V. (1987). The principle of contrast: A constraint on language acquisition. In B. MacWhinney (Ed.), *Mechanisms of language acquisition* (pp. 1–33). Hillsdale, NJ: Erlbaum.

Conkright, L., Flannagan, D., & Dykes, J. (2000). Effects of pronoun type and gender role consistency on children's recall and interpretation of stories. *Sex Roles, 43*, 481–497.

Cordua, G. D., McGraw, K. O., & Drabman, R. S. (1979). Doctor or nurse: Children's perception of sex typed occupations. *Child Development, 50*, 590–593.

Crawford, M. (2001). Gender and language. In R. K. Unger (Ed.), *Handbook of the psychology of women and gender* (pp. 228–244). New York: John Wiley & Sons.

Crowley, K., Callanan, M. A., Tenenbaum, H. R., & Allen, E. (2001). Parents explain more often to boys than to girls during shared scientific thinking. *Psychological Science, 12*, 258–261.

Darrow, W. (1970). *I'm glad I'm a boy, I'm glad I'm a girl!* New York: Simon & Schuster.

Deák, G. O., & Maratsos, M. (1998). On having complex representations of things: Preschoolers use multiple words for objects and people. *Developmental Psychology, 34*, 224–240.

DeLoache, J. S., Cassidy, D. J., & Carpenter, C. J. (1987). The three bears are all boys: Mothers' gender labeling of neutral picture book characters. *Sex Roles, 17*, 163–178.

DeLoache, J. S., & DeMendoza, O. A. P. (1987). Joint picturebook interactions of mothers and 1-year-old children. *British Journal of Developmental Psychology, 5*, 111–123.

Dunn, J., Bretherton, I., & Munn, P. (1987). Conversations about feeling states between mothers and their young children. *Developmental Psychology, 23*, 132–139.

Edelbrock, C., & Sugawara, A. I. (1978). Acquisition of sex-typed preferences in preschool-aged children. *Developmental Psychology*, **14**, 614–623.

Eichstedt, J. A., Serbin, L. A., Poulin-Dubois, D., & Sen, M. G. (2002). Of bears and men: Infants' knowledge of conventional and metaphorical gender stereotypes. *Infant Behavior & Development*, **25**, 296–310.

Eisenberg, N., Wolchick, S. A., Hernandez, R., & Pasternack, J. F. (1985). Parental socialization of young children's play: A short-term longitudinal study. *Child Development*, **56**, 1506–1513.

Fagot, B. I. (1977). Consequences of moderate cross-gender behavior in preschool children. *Child Development*, **48**, 902–907.

Fagot, B. I. (1978). Reinforcing contingencies for sex-role behaviors: Effect of experience with children. *Child Development*, **49**, 30–36.

Fagot, B. I., & Hagan, R. (1991). Observations of parent reactions to sex-stereotyped behaviors: Age and sex effects. *Child Development*, **62**, 617–628.

Fagot, B. I., Hagan, R., Leinbach, M. D., & Krosenberg, S. (1985). Differential reactions to assertive and communicative acts of toddler boys and girls. *Child Development*, **56**, 1499–1505.

Fagot, B. I., & Leinbach, M. D. (1995). Gender knowledge in egalitarian and traditional families. *Sex Roles*, **32**, 513–526.

Fivush, R. (1989). Exploring sex differences in the emotional content of mother-child conversations about the past. *Sex Roles*, **20**, 675–691.

Gastil, J. (1990). Generic pronouns and sexist language: The oxymoronic character of masculine generics. *Sex Roles*, **23**, 629–643.

Gelman, S. A. (2003). *The essential child: Origins of essentialism in everyday thought*. New York: Oxford University Press.

Gelman, S. A., Coley, J. D., Rosengren, K., Hartman, E., & Pappas, T. (1998). Beyond labeling: The role of parental input in the acquisition of richly-structured categories. *Monographs of the Society for Research in Child Development* (Serial No. 253, Vol. 63(1)). Boston, MA: Blackwell.

Gelman, S. A., Collman, P., & Maccoby, E. E. (1986). Inferring properties from categories versus inferring categories from properties: The case of gender. *Child Development*, **57**, 396–404.

Gelman, S. A., & Heyman, G. D. (1999). Carrot-eaters and creature-believers: The effects of lexicalization on children's inferences about social categories. *Psychological Science*, **10**, 489–493.

Gelman, S. A., & Markman, E. M. (1986). Categories and induction in young children. *Cognition*, **23**, 183–209.

Gelman, S. A., & Taylor, M. G. (2000). Gender essentialism in cognitive development. In P. H. Miller & E. K. Scholnick (Eds.), *Developmental psychology through the lenses of feminist theories* (pp. 169–190). London: Routledge.

Gentile, D. A. (1993). Just what are sex and gender, anyway? A call for a new terminological standard. *Psychological Science*, **4**, 120–122.

Gentner, D., & Goldin-Meadow, S. (Eds.) (2003). *Language in mind: Advances in the study of language and thought*. Cambridge, MA: MIT Press.

Gentner, D., & Namy, L. L. (2000). Comparison in the development of categories. *Cognitive Development*, **14**, 487–513.

Gleason, J. B. (1987). Sex differences in parent–child interaction. In S. U. Philips, S. Steele & C. Tanz (Eds.), *Language, gender, and sex in comparative perspective* (pp. 189–199). New York: Cambridge University Press.

Gopnik, A., Choi, S., & Baumberger, T. (1996). Cross-linguistic differences in early semantic and cognitive development. *Cognitive Development*, **11**, 197–227.

Gottfried, G. M., & Tonks, S. J. M. (1996). Specifying the relation between novel and known: Input affects the acquisition of novel color terms. *Child Development*, **67**, 850–866.

Graddol, D., & Swann, J. (1989). *Gender voices*. Cambridge, MA: Blackwell.

Greenwald, A. G., & Banaji, M. R. (1995). Implicit social cognition: Attitudes, self-esteem, and stereotypes. *Psychological Review*, **102**, 4–27.

Hall, D. G., & Waxman, S. R. (1993). Assumptions about word meaning: Individuation and basic-level kinds. *Child Development*, **64**, 1550–1570.

Haslam, N., Rothschild, L., & Ernst, D. (2002). Are essentialist beliefs associated with prejudice? *British Journal of Social Psychology*, **41**, 87–100.

Hendrick, J., & Stange, T. (1991). Do actions speak louder than words? An effect of the functional use of language on dominant sex role behavior in boys and girls. *Early Childhood Research Quarterly*, **6**, 565–576.

Henley, N. M. (1989). Molehill or mountain? What we know and don't know about sex bias in language. In M. Crawford & M. Gentry (Eds.), *Gender and thought: Psychological perspectives* (pp. 59–78). New York: Springer-Verlag.

Heyman, G. D., & Gelman, S. A. (2000). Preschool children's use of trait labels to make inductive inferences. *Journal of Experimental Child Psychology*, **77**, 1–19.

Heyman, G., & Gelman, S. A. (1999). The use of trait labels in making psychological inferences. *Child Development*, **70**, 604–619.

Hollander, M. A., Gelman, S. A., & Star, J. (2002). Children's interpretation of generic noun phrases. *Developmental Psychology*, **38**, 883–894.

Hort, B. E., Fagot, B. I., & Leinbach, M. D. (1990). Are people's notions of maleness more stereotypically framed than their notions of femaleness? *Sex Roles*, **23**, 197–212.

Hort, B. E., Leinbach, M. D., & Fagot, B. I. (1991). Is there coherence among components of gender acquisition? *Sex Roles*, **24**, 195–208.

Hyde, J. S. (1984). Children's understanding of sexist language. *Developmental Psychology*, **20**, 697–706.

Imai, M., & Gentner, D. (1997). A crosslinguistic study of early word meaning: Universal ontology and linguistic influence. *Cognition*, **62**, 169–200.

Johnston, K. E., Madole, K. L., Bittinger, K., & Smith, A. (2001). Developmental changes in infants' and toddlers' attention to gender categories. *Merrill-Palmer Quarterly*, **47**, 563–584.

Karmiloff-Smith, A. (1977). More about the same: Children's understanding of post-articles. *Journal of Child Language*, **4**, 377–394.

Katz, P. A. (1986). Modification of children's gender-stereotyped behavior: General issues and research considerations. *Sex Roles*, **14**, 591–602.

Katz, P. A. (1996). Raising feminists. *Psychology of Women Quarterly*, **20**, 323–340.

Katz, P. A., & Ksansak, K. R. (1994). Developmental aspects of gender role flexibility and traditionality in middle childhood and adolescence. *Developmental Psychology*, **30**, 272–282.

Killen, M., Pisacane, K., Lee-Kim, J., & Ardila-Rey, A. (2001). Fairness of stereotypes? Young children's priorities when evaluating group exclusion and inclusion. *Developmental Psychology*, **37**, 587–596.

Koblinsky, S. G., Cruse, D. F., & Sugawara, A. I. (1978). Sex role stereotypes and children's memory for story content. *Child Development*, **49**, 452–458.

Kuhn, D., Nash, S., & Brucken, L. (1978). Sex role concepts of two- and three-year-olds. *Child Development*, **49**, 445–451.

Kuebli, J., Butler, S., & Fivush, R. (1995). Mother-child talk about past emotions: Relations of maternal language and child gender over time. *Cognition and Emotion*, **9**, 265–283.

Leaper, C. (1994). *Exploring the consequences of gender segregation on social relationships. Childhood gender segregation: Causes and consequences. New directions for child development, No. 65* (pp. 67–86). San Francisco: Jossey-Bass/Pfeiffer.

Leaper, C. (2000). The social construction and socialization of gender during development. In P. H. Miller, & E. Kofsky Scholnick (Eds.), *Toward a feminist developmental psychology* (pp. 127–152). Florence, KY: Taylor & Francis/Routledge.

Leaper, C. (2002). Parenting girls and boys. In M. H. Bornstein (Ed.), *Handbook of parenting: Vol. 1: Children and parenting* (2nd ed., pp. 189–225). Mahwah, NJ: Lawrence Erlbaum Associates, Publishers.

Leaper, C., Anderson, K. J., & Sanders, P. (1998). Moderators of gender effects on parents' talk to their children: A meta-analysis. *Developmental Psychology, 34,* 3–27.

Leinbach, M. D., & Fagot, B. I. (1986). Acquisition of gender labels: A test for toddlers. *Sex Roles, 15,* 655–667.

Leinbach, M. D., & Fagot, B. I. (1993). Categorical habituation to male and female faces: Gender schematic processing in infancy. *Infant Behavior and Development, 16,* 317–332.

Lemm, K., & Banaji, M. R. (1999). Unconscious attitudes and beliefs about women and men. In U. Pasero & F. Braun (Eds.), *Wahrnehmung und Herstellung von Geschlecht (Perceiving and performing gender)* (pp. 215–233). Opladen: Westdutscher Verlag.

Levy, G. D. (1999). Gender-typed and non-gender-typed category awareness in toddlers. *Sex Roles, 41,* 851–873.

Levy, G. D., & Haaf, R. A. (1994). Detection of gender-related categories by 10-month-old infants. *Infant Behavior and Development, 17,* 457–459.

Levy, G. D., Taylor, M. G., & Gelman, S. A. (1995). Traditional and evaluative aspects of flexibility in gender roles, social conventions, moral rules, and physical laws. *Child Development, 66,* 515–531.

Liben, L. S., & Bigler, R. S. (2002). The developmental course of gender differentiation: Conceptualizing, measuring, and evaluating constructs and pathways. *Monographs of the Society for Research in Child Development, 67*(2). Boston, MA: Blackwell.

Liben, L. S., Bigler, R. S., & Krogh, H. R. (2002). Language at work: Children's gendered interpretations of occupational titles. *Child Development, 73,* 810–828.

Liben, L. S., & Signorella, M. L. (Eds.) (1987). *Children's gender schemata. (New directions for child development, No. 38.).* San Francisco: Jossey-Bass.

Liben, L. S., & Signorella, M. L. (1980). Gender-related schemata and constructive memory in children. *Child Development, 51,* 11–18.

Lyons, J. (1977). *Semantics* (**Vol. 1**). New York: Cambridge University Press.

Lytton, H., & Romney, D. M. (1991). Parents' differential socialization of boys and girls: A meta-analysis. *Psychological Bulletin, 109,* 267–296.

Maccoby, E. E. (1988). Gender as a social category. *Developmental Psychology, 24,* 755–765.

Maccoby, E. E. (1998). *The two sexes: Growing up apart, coming together.* Cambridge, MA: Belknap/Harvard.

Maccoby, E. E. (2002). The intersection of nature and socialization in childhood gender development. In C. von Hofsten & L. Baeckman (Eds.), *Psychology at the turn of the millennium, Vol. 2: Social, developmental, and clinical perspectives* (pp. 37–52). Florence, KY: Taylor & Frances/Routledge.

MacKay, D. G. (1980). Psychology, prescriptive grammar, and the pronoun problem. *American Psychologist, 35,* 444–449.

MacWhinney, B., & Snow, C. (1990). The child language data exchange system: An update. *Journal of Child Language, 17,* 457–472.

Mahalingam, R. (1998). *Essentialism, power, and representation of caste: A developmental study.* Ph.D. dissertation, University of Pittsburgh.

Markman, A. B., & Gentner, D. (2000). Structure mapping in the comparison process. *American Journal of Psychology, 113,* 501–538.

Markman, E. M. (1989). *Categorization and naming in children: Problems in induction.* Cambridge: Bradford Book/MIT Press.

Martin, C. L. (1989). Children's use of gender related information in making social judgments. *Developmental Psychology*, **25**, 80–88.

Martin, C. L., Eisenbud, L., & Rose, H. (1995). Children's gender-based reasoning about toys. *Child Development*, **66**, 1453–1471.

Martin, C. L., & Halverson, C. F. (1983). Gender constancy: A methodological and theoretical analysis. *Sex Roles*, **9**, 775–790.

Martin, C. L., Ruble, D. N., & Szkrybalo, J. (2002). Cognitive theories of early gender development. *Psychological Bulletin*, **128**, 903–933.

Medin, D. (1989). Concepts and conceptual structure. *American Psychologist*, **44**, 1469–1481.

Montemayor, R. (1974). Children's performance in a game and their attraction to it as a function of sex-typed labels. *Child Development*, **45**, 152–156.

Murphy, C. M. (1978). Pointing in the context of a shared activity. *Child Development*, **49**, 371–380.

Nguyen, S. P., & Murphy, G. L. (2003). An apple is more than a fruit: Cross-classification in children's concepts. *Child Development*, **74**, 1783–1806.

Ninio, A. (1980). Ostensive definition in vocabulary teaching. *Journal of Child Language*, **7**, 565–573.

Ochs, E., & Schieffelin, B. B. (1984). Language acquisition and socialization: Three developmental stories and their implications. In R. A. Shweder & R. A. LeVine (Eds.), *Culture theory: Essays on mind, self, and emotion* (pp. 276–320). New York: Cambridge University Press.

Pappas, A., & Gelman, S. A. (1998). Generic noun phrases in mother-child conversations. *Journal of Child Language*, **25**, 19–33.

Poulin-Dubois, D., Serbin, L. A., & Derbyshire, A. (1998). Toddlers' intermodal and verbal knowledge. *Merrill-Palmer Quarterly*, **44**, 339–354.

Poulin-Dubois, D., Serbin, L. A., Kenyon, B., & Derbyshire, A. (1994). Infants' intermodal knowledge about gender. *Developmental Psychology*, **30**, 436–442.

Powlishta, K. K., Sen, M. G., Serbin, L. A., Poulin-Dubois, D., & Eichstedt, J. A. (2001). From infancy through middle childhood: The role of cognitive and social factors in becoming gendered. In R. K. Unger (Ed.), *Handbook of women and gender* (pp. 116–132). New York: Wiley.

Prasada, S. (2000). Acquiring generic knowledge. *Trends in Cognitive Sciences*, **4**, 66–72.

Quine, W. V. (1960). *Word and object*. Cambridge, MA: MIT Press.

Rehder, B., & Hastie, R. (2001). Causal knowledge and categories: The effects of causal beliefs on categorization, induction, and similarity. *Journal of Experimental Psychology: General*, **130**, 323–360.

Rozin, P., Ashmore, M., & Markwith, M. (1996). Lay American conceptions of nutrition: Dose insensitivity, categorical thinking, contagion, and the monotonic mind. *Health Psychology*, **15**, 438–447.

Ruble, D. N., Balaban, T., & Cooper, J. (1981). Gender constancy and the effects of sex-typed televised toy commercials. *Child Development*, **52**, 667–673.

Ruble, D. N., & Martin, C. L. (1998). Gender development. In W. Damon (Series Ed.) & N. Eisenberg (Ed.), *Handbook of child psychology: Vol. 3. Social, emotional, and personality development* (5th ed., pp. 933–1016). New York: Wiley.

Sabbagh, M. A., & Callanan, M. A. (1998). Metarepresentation in action: 3-, 4-, and 5-year-olds' developing theories of mind in parent-child conversations. *Developmental Psychology*, **34**, 491–502.

Scarr, S., & McCartney, K. (1983). How people make their own environments: A theory of genotype-environment effects. *Child Development*, **54**, 424–435.

Serbin, L. A., Poulin-Dubois, D., Colburne, K. A., Sen, M. G., & Eichstedt, J. A. (2001). Gender stereotyping in infancy: Visual preferences for and knowledge of gender-stereotyped toys in the second year. *International Journal of Behavioral Development*, **25**, 7–15.

Serbin, L. A., & Sprafkin, C. (1986). The salience of gender and the process of sex typing in three- to seven-year-old children. *Child Development*, **57**, 1188–1199.

Shatz, M., & Wilcox, S. A. (1991). Constraints on the acquisition of English modals. In S. A. Gelman & J. P. Byrnes (Eds.), *Perspectives on language and thought: Interrelations in development* (pp. 319–353). New York: Cambridge University Press.

Shatz, M. (1994). *A toddler's life: Becoming a person*. New York: Oxford University Press.

Shatz, M., Wellman, H. M., & Silber, S. (1983). The acquisition of mental verbs: A systematic investigation of the first reference to mental state. *Cognition*, **14**, 301–321.

Siegal, M. (1987). Are sons and daughters treated more differently by fathers than mothers? *Developmental Review*, **7**, 183–209.

Signorella, M. L., Bigler, R. S., & Liben, L. S. (1993). Developmental differences in children's gender schemata about others: A meta-analytic review. *Developmental Review*, **13**, 147–183.

Signorella, M. L., Bigler, R. S., & Liben, L. S. (1997). A meta-analysis of children's memories for own-sex and other-sex information. *Journal of Applied Developmental Psychology*, **18**, 429–445.

Signorella, M. L., & Liben, L. S. (1984). Recall and reconstruction of gender-related pictures: Effects of attitude, task difficulty, and age. *Child Development*, **55**, 393–405.

Signorielli, N., & Bacue, A. (1999). Recognition and respect: A content analysis of prime-time television characters across three decades. *Sex Roles*, **40**, 527–544.

Snow, C. E. (1972). Mothers' speech to children learning language. *Child Development*, **43**, 549–565.

Snow, C. E., & Goldfield, B. A. (1983). Turn the page please: Situation-specific language acquisition. *Journal of Child Language*, **10**, 551–569.

Snow, M. E., Jacklin, C. N., & Maccoby, E. E. (1983). Sex-of-child differences in father-child interaction at one year of age. *Child Development*, **54**, 227–232.

Sroufe, L. A., Bennett, C., Englund, M., & Urban, J. (1993). The significance of gender boundaries in preadolescence: Contemporary correlates and antecedents of boundary violation and maintenance. *Child Development*, **64**, 455–466.

Stangor, C., & Ruble, D. N. (1989). Differential influences of gender schemata and gender constancy on children's information processing and behavior. *Social Cognition*, **7**, 353–372.

Stipek, D. J., Gralinski, J. H., & Kopp, C. B. (1990). Self-concept development in the toddler years. *Developmental Psychology*, **26**, 972–977.

Switzer, J. Y. (1990). The impact of generic word choices: An empirical investigation of age- and sex-related differences. *Sex Roles*, **22**, 69–82.

Tabachnick, B. G., & Fidell, L. S. (1989). *Using multivariate statistics*. Philadelphia, PA: Harper & Row.

Taylor, M. G. (1996). The development of children's beliefs about social and biological aspects of gender differences. *Child Development*, **67**, 1555–1571.

Taylor, M. G., & Gelman, S. A. (1993). Children's gender- and age-based categorization in similarity and induction tasks. *Social Development*, **2**, 104–121.

Tenenbaum, H. R., & Leaper, C. (2002). Are parents' gender schemas related to their children's gender-related cognitions? A meta-analysis. *Developmental Psychology*, **38**, 615–630.

Thorne, B., & Luria, Z. (1986). Sexuality and gender in children's daily worlds. *Social Problems*, **33**, 176–190.

Unger, R. K. (1979). Toward a redefinition of sex and gender. *American Psychologist*, **34**, 1085–1094.

Van Kleeck, A., Stahl, S. A., & Bauer, E. B. (Eds.) (2003). *On reading books to children: Parents and teachers*. Mahwah, NJ: Erlbaum.

Waugh, L. R. (1982). Marked and unmarked: A choice between unequals in semiotic structure. *Semiotica*, **38**, 299–318.

Waxman, S. R. (1999). The dubbing ceremony revisited: Object naming and categorization in infancy and early childhood. In D. L. Medin & S. Atran (Eds.), *Folkbiology* (pp. 233–284). Cambridge, MA: MIT Press.

Waxman, S. R., & Klibanoff, R. S. (2000). The role of comparison in the extension of novel adjectives. *Developmental Psychology, 36*, 571–581.

Waxman, S. R., & Markow, D. B. (1995). Words as invitations to form categories: Evidence from 12- to 13-month-old infants. *Cognitive Psychology, 29*, 257–302.

Weisner, T. S., & Wilson-Mitchell, J. E. (1990). Nonconventional family life-styles and sex typing in 6-year-olds. *Child Development, 61*, 1915–1933.

Weitzman, N., Birns, B., & Friend, R. (1985). Traditional and nontraditional mothers' communication with their daughters and sons. *Child Development, 56*, 894–898.

Welder, A. N., & Graham, S. A. (2001). The influence of shape similarity and shared labels on infants' inductive inferences about nonobvious object properties. *Child Development, 72*, 1653–1673.

Wheeler, M. P. (1983). Context-related age changes in mothers' speech: Joint book reading. *Journal of Child Language, 10*, 259–263.

Whiting, B. B., & Edwards, C. P. (1988). *Children of different worlds: The formation of social behavior.* Cambridge, MA: Harvard University Press.

Xu, F. (1999). Object individuation and object identity in infancy: The role of spatiotemporal information, object property information, and language. *Acta Psychologica, 102*, 113–136.

Xu, F. (2002). The role of language in acquiring object kind concepts in infancy. *Cognition, 85*, 223–250.

ACKNOWLEDGMENTS

This research was supported by a grant from the Institute for Research on Women and Gender at the University of Michigan, and NICHD grant HD36043 to the first author. We are grateful to the families who participated in this research. We also thank Matthew Germak, Sonia Liu, Joanne Morgan, Kerry Kelly, and Laura Welch for their dedicated and conscientious work transcribing and/or coding the data. Thanks also to Matt Vendlinski, Rebekah Wolfman, Sarah Franke, Edith Kong, Denise Larabell, Bethany Gorka, Brook McCloud, and Felicia Kleinberg for assistance with tallying data, and Andrew Gelman for statistical advice. Correspondence should be addressed to: Susan Gelman, Department of Psychology, University of Michigan, 525 E. University Ave., Ann Arbor MI 48109-1109, e-mail: gelman@umich.edu.

COMMENTARY

GENDERED LANGUAGE AND SEXIST THOUGHT

Campbell Leaper and Rebecca S. Bigler

Gelman, Taylor, and Nguyen have carried out an impressive investigation into the socialization of gender during early childhood. That is, the researchers take a careful and detailed look at mothers' talk about gender to their children. The focus is on language that both reflects and fosters essentialist beliefs about gender. The authors also considered speech that challenges gender stereotypes. In doing so, they integrate and advance ideas within four research areas: gender socialization (e.g., Bussey & Bandura, 1999), children's concept development (e.g., Gelman, 2003), language and gender (e.g., Henley, 1989), and feminist psychology (e.g., Bohan, 1993).

Whereas many studies have previously examined gender-related variations in parents' language style with their children, there has not been a corresponding interest in examining how gender itself is referenced (see Raasch, Leaper, & Bigler, 2004, for an exception). Gelman and her colleagues have examined implicit ways that language defines gender through references to generic gender categories (e.g., "Girls play with dolls"), gender labeling (e.g., "That's a boy racing the car"), and gender contrasts (e.g., "That's for girls, not boys"). We believe that their work represents a significant advance in the field, especially for understanding the origins of gender typing. In our commentary, we note some of the important theoretical bases of the work, and highlight some of the findings that we feel are especially important. Throughout, we suggest avenues for future research. In our closing comments, we consider some implications of the research for changing gendered components of language and its use.

THEORETICAL FOUNDATIONS

The *Monograph* adopts one of several possible theoretical stances on the origins of gender typing, and more specifically, the role of language in shaping gender typing. Liben and Bigler (2002) outlined three broad families of theoretical approaches to understanding gender role development: essentialism, environmentalism, and constructivism. Gender essentialist explanations argue that most gender differences are innate and the product of evolutionary pressures that differed for males and females. Such theories view gendered language and sexist thought as the *products* of men's and women's inherently different natures. That is, neither gendered language, nor sexist thought, are viewed as important determinants of gender typing, or each other. According to this interpretation, gendered language evolved to reflect important differences in the world (e.g., gender is essentialist and, thus, so is the language used to speak about it); gender stereotypes are adaptive because they generally contain a "kernel of truth." Gelman and her co-authors do not adopt this theoretical stance, but neither do their data clearly refute such a position. We view their findings as most compatible with the other two families of explanation.

A second broad class of theories views gender typing as the result of social practices, referred to as gender environmentalism. For many decades, work within this tradition emphasized the role of operant conditioning (e.g., reinforcement), observational learning, and direct teaching in shaping gender development. Many researchers explored the role of language as a vehicle through which these mechanisms can operate. For example, verbal messages might be used to reinforce children's gender stereotypic behaviors. Indeed, many parents tend to openly encourage gender-typed activities in their children (see Leaper, 2002; Lytton & Romney, 1991). Researchers have also observed parents using language differently with girls and boys. For example, Leaper, Anderson, and Sanders (1998) found in their meta-analysis that mothers were more talkative, used more supportive speech, and more directive speech with daughters than with sons. Within the environmentalist theoretical paradigm, the focus was on the valence of messages (e.g., positive or negative reactions) or the way words are used (e.g., directive or supportive speech)—rather than the content of the words themselves (e.g., use of generics).

Gender environmentalist approaches, however, have fallen out of favor over the last two decades for many reasons. There is increasing evidence that environmental factors alone could not account for the extensive and rigid gender typing typical of early childhood. For example, children often make stereotypic statements ("Only boys like oysters") that were not taught to them or modeled by others. A second reason for the decline is that it became clear that cognitive factors were mediating the process of gender typing (e.g., Martin & Ruble, 2004). For example, for role models to have an impact, children must abstract the social category that particular models represent. They must further infer that the role model is representative of the social category (Perry & Bussey, 1979). As a result of these trends, many

129

researchers turned away from solely examining environmental influences on gender typing.

The work by Gelman and her colleagues is notable in that it is characterized, in part, by a gender environmentalist approach. The authors take a very detailed look at the linguistic input that children receive about gender. They examine, for example, whether mothers are (1) directly teaching children about the links between gender and various attributes (e.g., "Boys like to drive race cars") and (2) reinforcing or discouraging (via agreement or contradiction) children's gender-typed statements. That is, their analysis follows the tradition of much earlier work examining the consequences that children receive for their gender-typed or cross-gender-typed behavior (see Leaper, 2002). At the same time, the *Monograph* moves well beyond documenting instances of direct teaching and reinforcement, and includes components that are drawn from the third family of theories of gender differentiation.

The work by Gelman and her colleagues fits best within the family of theories that Liben and Bigler referred to as gender constructivism. Most contemporary theoretical approaches are constructivist in nature (see Bussey & Bandura, 1999; Leaper, 2000; Liben & Bigler, 2002; Martin, Ruble, & Szkrybalo, 2002). Constructivist theories reject the position that children are passive recipients of environmental messages (e.g., explicit messages) about gender. Instead, children are viewed as active agents who seek to extract and understand the important social categories in their environment. Thus, the environment is seen as only one source of information for constructing ideas about gender. The *Monograph* clearly reflects such a stance. Gelman and her colleagues do not propose that parents directly teach, or even reinforce, gender essentialist thinking. (One could, for example, imagine a mother commenting, "It's a girl. Girls are different in lots of very important ways from boys.") Instead, Gelman et al. claim that children construct gender categories that are characterized by essentialist elements, and that they do so *without explicit instruction* from their parents.

So why do children attend to gender and construct essentialist theories about gender? Gelman and colleagues believe that adult speakers provide children with important *implicit* messages about gender via the use of gender labels, gender contrasts, and generics; and that children use these cues in constructing theories about the meaning and importance of gender. Gelman et al.'s emphasis on children's developing gender concepts, and the relation between language and cognition, fits well with gender constructivists' emphasis on how children actively construct their understandings of gender, and how these concepts guide their behavior. At the same time, by pointing to the role of parents in transmitting these messages and providing evaluative responses, the research is compatible with the environmentalists' emphasis on the influences of direct teaching and feedback. As Gelman,

Taylor, and Nguyen (p. 93) state, "children's gender concepts are unlikely to be wholly self-generated, and instead are open to cultural and environmental influences."

RELATIONS BETWEEN GENDERED LANGUAGE AND SEXIST THOUGHT

During the last two decades, the study of language and gender has become a field of its own. Of particular relevance to the present *Monograph* is the work examining how gendered language affects thought (see Gentner & Loewenstein, 2002). To this end, some of these researchers have invoked the Whorfian hypothesis (i.e., language shapes thought). Words are concepts and having a word for something thereby affects how one thinks about the world. The weaker version of the Whorfian hypothesis softens the causal relationship between language and thought, and more generally argues that language and thought are correlated and likely influence one another (Khorsroshahi, 1989).

Some previous research supports the notion that the use of gendered language and having gender-stereotypic thoughts are reciprocally related. For example, studies show that the generic use of masculine pronouns ("he") and nouns ("man") tends to lead to male imagery in children's and adults' thinking (Henley, 1989; Hyde, 1984). Similarly, Liben, Bigler, and Krogh (2002) reported that occupational titles that are marked for gender (e.g., "policeman") are more likely to be viewed by children as being appropriate for only one gender than those that are unmarked (e.g., plumber). At the same time, gender attitudes appear to affect language use and interpretation. Liben et al. (2002) indicated that children with traditional attitudes were more likely to believe that occupational labels marked for gender (e.g., "policeman") apply mostly to men than were their more egalitarian peers. The work reported in the *Monograph* is consistent with the idea that gendered language shapes gender typing and simultaneously that gender typing shapes language use and comprehension.

It is important to note, however, that Gelman et al.'s research seeks to address the *causal* influences of maternal language on children's gender typing. That is, the authors believe that adults' gendered language determines, at least in part, why and how children come to think about gender. They argue that mothers' use of generics, for example, may cause their children to attend to gender and, further, to develop essentialist beliefs about gender. For example, a mother who states, "Girls play with dolls," in response to a picture depicting a girl with a doll reifies the stereotype that *only* girls play with dolls.

131

Highlighting a pervasive source for implicit gender socialization—that is, essentialist language—is perhaps the most significant contribution of the study. This subtle (but ubiquitous) form of gender socialization is likely to increase the salience of gender; lead children to believe that individuals of different genders have deep, nonobvious and substantive differences; and provide regular reminders to children about the roles, traits, and activities that girls and boys are supposed to demonstrate. Accordingly, generics and other implicit forms of gendered language essentialize gender and provide gender proscriptions.

Some of the findings reported in the *Monograph* are consistent with a causal interpretation. For example, there was an apparent developmental shift in whether the mother or the child was more likely to introduce generics. Among the younger children, generics were primarily introduced by the mothers. However, by the age of 4 years, children were introducing more generics than were mothers. Similarly, there is empirical evidence indicating that the generic use of the pronoun "he" or noun phrases using "man" might *cause* gender-biased thinking (see Henley, 1989; Hyde, 1984). As the authors note, however, the data reported in the *Monograph* are merely suggestive of a causal link. Future work should examine possible causal links between various forms of gendered language and gender-typed thinking. We offer a few directions for study.

Because the age range that we are considering—approximately between 2 and 4 years of age—is not very great, longitudinal studies are feasible, and they would be helpful in addressing possible causal influences. One research question is whether language shapes thought, or if thinking shapes how one uses language. (A third possibility is for a reciprocal influence between language and thought.) To consider if variations in parents' use of gendered language do affect children's developing gender concepts, it would be necessary first to examine if parents' speech predicts the onset of young children's gender stereotypes. In an analogous manner, longitudinal studies have been able to establish that the amount of maternal language input predicts children's later vocabulary growth (e.g., Huttenlocher, Haight, Bryk, Seltzer, & Lyons, 1991). Second, researchers may examine if there is a direct relation between the specific types of roles, traits, and activities referenced in parents' gendered speech and the specific stereotypes that children subsequently endorse. Third, longitudinal research could track age-related changes in children's gender-typed beliefs and later use of gendered language. In this way, researchers could examine whether the onset of more egalitarian attitudes is predictive of subsequent changes in children's language use. A challenge to testing these research questions, however, is that few (if any) children are exposed only to the speech of their parents. It is common for young children—even toddlers—to hear language from many sources including older siblings, daycare teachers, and television programs.

In addition to longitudinal designs, experimental work also would be useful. For example, the language used to introduce novel objects or roles could be systematically varied (e.g., using generics or specific terms), and children's subsequent levels of gender typing could be measured. For example, a variation on Bradbard, Martin, Endsley, and Halverson's (1986) classic gender study could be performed. These researchers randomly labeled novel objects as either "for girls" or "for boys." Children subsequently explored and later remembered details about objects if the objects were labeled for their own gender compared to the other gender. In an analogous manner, a researcher could take a novel toy labeled with a novel word (e.g., Akhtar, Carpenter, & Tomasello, 1996) and reference gender using generics (e.g., "Girls like to play with the toma") or nongenerics (e.g., "This girl likes to play with the toma"). After exposing children to statements like this, researchers could later assess children's beliefs about girls' and boys' preferences for these objects (see Martin, Eisenbud, & Rose, 1995). One methodological challenge, however, would be to disambiguate children's memories for what was said versus their actual endorsement of a new stereotype.

To underscore the potential impact of essentialist language in children's lives, the authors appropriately cited MacKay's (1980) insightful analysis of how sexist language functions as effective propaganda: Propaganda techniques are most successful when they occur frequently; they are covert and indirect (and thereby difficult to challenge); they begin appearing at an early age; and they are associated with high-prestige sources (e.g., parents). We agree with this view. It is likely that children hear generic references to gender throughout each day and across home and school settings (Leaper, 1995a; Lloyd & Duveen, 1992). In their analysis of preschool classrooms, for example, Lloyd and Duveen (1992) observed that the teachers regularly used generic language to refer to girls and boys. Moreover, these were not teachers who endorsed traditional notions of gender. They openly professed their desire to avoid sexism. Nonetheless, the researchers observed that "the class teacher's most common way of employing gender-group membership and highlighting social categories was by invoking the terms 'girls' or 'boys', either singly or together, to organize classroom activity... She called out 'boys' to tell children, usually the same particular boys, to stop running around, to calm down and to be careful, a comment on their behavioural style..." (p. 65). In thinking about the possible impact of such language, it is useful to imagine a world in which similar speech patterns were applied to race. Most individuals readily predict that the routine use of racial labels ("Good morning, Whites and Latinos") would result in increased levels of racial stereotyping and prejudice (see Bigler, 1995).

In summary, Gelman, Taylor, and Nguyen's research suggests that the relation between language and thought may be complicated. On the one

133

hand, there was some indication that mothers' and children's gender-related cognitions were related to their respective uses of gendered language. This finding is consistent with some prior research indicating that women with feminist attitudes are less likely than other women to use sexist language (Jacobson & Insko, 1985; Matheson & Kristiansen, 1987). In this way, a link between language and thought is implicated. However, what seems more compelling was that mothers who endorsed egalitarian gender attitudes typically affirmed children's stereotypes and often used generic statements in their speech. The latter set of findings imply a disconnection between the mothers' thoughts and their speech. The reasons for such a disconnection are discussed in the following section.

RELATIONS AMONG MOTHERS' AND CHILDREN'S ATTITUDES AND BEHAVIOR

Gelman, Taylor, and Nguyen's data give us several interesting glimpses into the manner in which mothers socialize their children's beliefs about gender. We highlight a few of those findings here. It is first important to note that, overall, the mothers in the sample explicitly endorsed egalitarian gender attitudes. Specifically, they stated that *both* men and women should perform over 80% of the 71 gender-typed activities and occupations about which they were asked. At the same time, their children endorsed gender-stereotypic attitudes, as reflected in their responses to the stereotyping scale and spontaneous comments about gender. Thus, here as in other research, children's and their mothers' gender attitudes were not strongly related (see Tenenbaum & Leaper, 2002).

Despite the fact that the majority of mothers could be classified as having egalitarian beliefs, they appear to do little to inculcate such beliefs in their children. When children in the sample made stereotype-consistent statements, their mothers' most common response was to affirm the children's statement. Mothers explicitly negated their children's stereotype-consistent statements less than 3% of the time. Why were negations so infrequent in occurrence?

One possibility is that mothers, even feminist ones, make little attempt to socialize their young children to endorse similar beliefs. There are several possible motivations that might drive mothers with egalitarian views to keep their views to themselves. First, egalitarian mothers may *want* their children to become *knowledgeable* about the cultural stereotypes of gender and may do little, therefore, to interfere with their young children's accumulation of gender stereotype knowledge. That is, parents may believe that ignorance about gender stereotypes will lead children to look dumb in front of peers (e.g., a boy who announces to his kindergarten class that men can wear nail polish), or even to violate gender norms themselves and risk ridicule by their peers (e.g., a boy who wears nail polish to kindergarten).

Second, feminist mothers may assume that young children are *incapable* of understanding the environmental factors that produce skewed distributions of males and females into various traits and roles (including gender discrimination) and, thus, are reluctant to contradict the gender stereotypic statements of young children. These same mothers may begin to challenge their children's gender-typed beliefs when their children are older. Indeed, Gelman et al. did find that mothers were significantly more likely to challenge stereotype affirmations by 4- and 6-year-olds (3–4%) than those by 2-year-olds (less than 1%).

Third, mothers with egalitarian or feminist beliefs may be opposed by other family members, such as fathers and grandparents, in the goal of raising nonsexist children. Generally, studies indicate that fathers are more rigid in their gender typing of children, especially of sons, than are mothers (see Leaper, 2002). Fathers may prevail upon mothers to minimize their nonsexist teaching. Future research should ask mothers and fathers about their goals with respect to nonsexist child rearing, including their strategies for communicating their beliefs to their children.

A final reason we propose for why mothers may have been so unlikely to challenge children's gender stereotypes—and to be so likely to use generics themselves—is that many women may hold *contradictory* gender attitudes. Research on implicit stereotyping and prejudice suggests that people's conscious and unconscious attitudes are sometimes discrepant (Brauer, Wasel, & Niedenthal, 2000; Cunningham, Preacher, & Banaji, 2001). For example, a person who openly endorses racial equality may show signs of racial prejudice in a reaction-time paradigm (Fazio, Jackson, Dunton, & Williams, 1995). In an analogous manner, many mothers who consciously endorse gender-egalitarian ideals may harbor some traditional attitudes. Some support for such a notion is reported in the *Monograph*. Mothers typically offered few explicit stereotyped statements themselves. However, when implicit statements were analyzed, they occurred with high frequency in mothers' speech. Almost every mother in the sample (96%) made at least one generic statement about gender. Similarly, mothers were extremely likely (89%) to use at least one gender-ostensive labeling comment, and most (64%) mothers made at least one gender contrast. We do not mean to imply that these mothers are being disingenuous when they endorse gender-egalitarian views. On the contrary, we expect that many mothers *simultaneously* endorse genuinely egalitarian explicit beliefs about gender *and* hold more sexist implicit beliefs about gender. Accordingly, a critical goal of consciousness-raising groups is to increase participants' awareness of the many forms of bias that can be unconsciously perpetuated (Marecek & Hare-Mustin, 1991).

Another finding related to the endorsement of contradictory gender attitudes is notable. Gelman and colleagues found a greater incidence of both gender-stereotyped and gender-egalitarian beliefs among older children in their sample. That is, by age 6, children seemed to be developing contradictory beliefs about gender. Accordingly, Gelman and her co-authors point out that knowledge and beliefs cannot be characterized along a single dimension of stereotyping. By way of example, they cite Killen, Pisacane, Lee-Kim, and Ardila-Rey's (2001) work showing that children's gendered beliefs differ depending on their applications of moral versus social–conventional reasoning. We believe examining if and how children (and adults) can hold contradictory beliefs about gender is an intriguing topic for further study.

Despite the dissimilarities in their explicit gender attitudes, mothers' and children's language showed several important similarities. For example, significant correlations were seen between mothers' and children's use of generics ($r = .48$), gender-egalitarian statements ($r = .63$), and gender-ostensive labeling ($r = .78$). Correlations between conversational partners in language style are often found. Indeed, it is a basic principle of communication accommodation theory that partners' styles of communication will converge during a conversation (Coupland, Coupland, Giles, & Henwood, 1988). It is also a fundamental premise of the sociocultural theory of child development (e.g., Rogoff, 1990) that activity settings influence the types of behavior that are enacted (also see Leaper, 2000). In the present study, both mother and child were reading the same picture book together. Hence, it was likely they would refer to and discuss the same material. The influence of the activity context is further underscored by the impact of page type on the participants' speech. Gender affirmations were more likely during gender-stereotyped pages and egalitarian statements were more likely when reading counter-stereotyped pages.

Two implications of these findings follow. First, children and parents are likely to reinforce one another's speech styles. Hence, with younger children especially, parents may play an important role in guiding the kinds of concepts they develop and practice. But as children form their own ideas about gender, they may make it more difficult for parents to redirect them to alternative ways of thinking—especially if parents are reluctant to challenge their children's stereotypes (as tended to occur in the present study). A second implication is that the type of materials that we provide children matters. Books that present counter-stereotyped gender images are more likely to elicit comments that challenge traditional stereotypes. We would further underscore the importance of *counter-stereotypical* images rather than only neutral images. Prior research suggests that neutral images (e.g., gender-nonspecific animals) are often interpreted in gender-biased ways by children (Lambdin, Greer, Jibotian, Wood, & Hamilton, 2003) as well as parents (DeLoache, Cassidy, & Carpenter, 1987). Unfortunately, media that present counter-stereotypic images are rare. Moreover, children are swamped by an exhaustive catalogue of older "classic" materials, including books and television programming, that are highly gender typed.

Another notable finding pertains to mothers' tendency to respond differently to positive valence stereotypes (e.g., "Boys are race car drivers") versus negative valence stereotypes ("Girls can't be race car drivers"). Gelman and her colleagues raise interesting questions about the difference between these two types of statements. Do children understand negative valence statements as more informative about gender stereotypes than positive valence statements? Are children more likely to make generalizations from one type of statement more than the other? Positive valence statements are more pervasive in children's daily lives. However, negative valence comments may have more salience than do positive valence statements (e.g., Rosen & Grandison, 1994). Such statements may have an especially strong impact when a child's behavior is at odds with gender norms, and thus may trigger feelings of shame or embarrassment. For instance, hearing his father say, "Boys don't cry," may be more memorable for a boy than hearing his father say, "Boys are good at tools."

The research further showed that boys were more likely than girls to make negative valence statements and to express more generics. These results are consistent with the view that gender boundaries are more rigid for males than for females (see Leaper, 1994). According to a social identity interpretation, boys have more at stake than girls in maintaining group boundaries due to males' higher status in society (see Leaper, 1994). There is also a psychoanalytic explanation that proposes that boys' early gender identity tends to be defined in negative terms (see Chodorow, 1978). As argued, because women are typically primary caregivers, boys tend to define their gender identity as "not-female." Both of these interpretations could be tested in future research. To test whether higher-status group members are more likely to use generics to define group boundaries, researchers could compare the speech of high- and low-status groups that are experimentally assigned (e.g., Bigler, Brown, & Markell, 2001). Alternatively, to test if access to same-gender role models is important during early childhood, researchers could examine boys' use of generics when their primary caregivers are fathers versus mothers.

Mothers' frequent use of gender-essentialist language may be interpreted as contradicting the view that parents play a minimal role during gender socialization (e.g., Lytton & Romney, 1991; Maccoby & Jacklin, 1974). Gelman and her colleagues found that parents did not often express gender stereotypes in their explicit speech. But this contrasted with mothers' implicit speech which often reinforced gender-stereotyped notions. Moreover, mothers typically provided positive responses to

137

children's own affirmations of gender stereotypes. In sum, despite most of these mothers' egalitarian attitudes, they were contributing to children's gender-stereotyped views of the world.

CHANGING THE LEXICON AND ITS USES

To those individuals who are committed to gender-egalitarian ideals—such as raising children to be nonsexist or feminist—the results presented in the *Monograph* are likely to be troubling. The notion that common and widely accepted patterns of language (e.g., use of generics) may facilitate children's essentialist thinking about gender suggests that it may be important to alter aspects of our language to combat such tendencies.

There has been some significant progress in altering the lexicon to remove sexist components of language. Over the years, for example, there has been a shift in people's speech and writing away from the generic use of the masculine pronouns "he" and masculine compound nouns such as "chairman." Instead, it is now common to find people using gender-inclusive language such as "he or she" or "chairperson" (Rubin, Greene, & Schneider, 1994). The American Psychological Association made its own contribution by banning sexist language in its publications (American Psychological Association Publication Manual Task Force, 1977). However, it is probably easier to be mindful of words that exclude one gender (i.e., the generic use of masculine pronouns) than it is to be aware of one's use of generic phrases to refer to girls and boys (or to women and men). Ironically, authors of psychology studies frequently make statements that refer to gender using generics (e.g., "Women scored higher on the measure than did men"). Gelman and her colleagues, for example, state "boys provided more negative valence talk than [did] girls" (p. 138). (We are guilty of making similar statements in our own publications.) Just as children may translate generics into stereotypic beliefs, the lay public often interprets generic statements by researchers as evidence that women and men (or girls and boys) differ in important, clear, and consistent ways. In other words, the use of generics probably biases individuals to attend to between-gender differences and ignore within-gender variability. One way to address this problem is to make more effort to include qualifiers in our writing (e.g., "*On the average*, the women in our sample scored higher than did the men"). Also, we should regularly reiterate that average gender differences are typically associated with a high degree of overlap.

A more radical solution would be to call for changes to the lexicon aimed at minimizing the "lexicalization" of gender. Theoretically, several reforms are possible. For example, we might move to abolish gender-marked pronouns (e.g., "he," "she") within the English language and adopt a truly neutral form (see MacKay, 1980), as occurs in some languages such as Turkish (see Graddol & Swann, 1989, p. 128). Additionally, the use of nouns (e.g., "girl," "boy," "man," "woman") that mark gender could be discouraged. Interestingly, there appears to have been just such a movement concerning race and ethnicity. Whereas use of terms such as "Negro" or "Jew" were common, we now prefer adjectives to describe race and ethnicity (as well as other forms of status such as sexual orientation and ability). For example, the statement "My neighbor is Jewish" is less offensive to some listeners than the statement "My neighbor is a Jew." Finally, some writers (Leaper, 1995b; Lott, 1981) have argued against social scientists' use of the terms "feminine" and "masculine" to describe behaviors on the grounds that such terms are essentialist. That is, the terms suggest that certain behaviors are inherently female-like or male-like—as opposed to human qualities that everyone can potentially share.

There have, in fact, been calls to bar the use of race as an adjective when describing individuals. A recent billboard in Austin, Texas read, "He is a very articulate black man" with a red line through the term "black." The billboard was trying to make a point about the irrelevance of the person's race. Paradoxically, however, the editorial change removed the reference to race and left not one but *two* markers for gender ("he" and "man"). Alternatively, the billboard could have stated "That is a very articulate person."

Less radically, we suggest that, ideally, parents should refrain from labeling gender when it is not necessary. But this is difficult to achieve. As discussed earlier, people's attitudes and behavior do not always match. We can offer a personal anecdote that illustrates this point. The first author has noticed that the second author often refers to her two daughters as "the girls" (rather than by their names). This occurs despite the second author endorsing feminist attitudes. Moreover, the same author has even argued against teachers referring to students in their classrooms as "boys and girls" because it reinforces unnecessary and irrelevant gender divisions (see Bigler, 1995). Old habits die hard, even for some feminists (see Leaper, 1995a).

Finally, it is worth noting that there is an important paradox inherent in the processes of fighting sexism. The goal of many individuals is to minimize the use of gender as an important social category (i.e., the use of gender for assigning traits and roles). But to explain why gender distributions are skewed (i.e., all of the Presidents of the United States have been male) requires that gender be addressed explicitly. So, Gelman and her co-authors report that when discussing stereotype-inconsistent pages, mothers were more likely to make stereotype-inconsistent remarks and *simultaneously* to emphasize gender via the use of generics (e.g., "Girls can be fire fighters"). Ironically, they note that the process of highlighting gender (via generics) may impede the goal that the statement was aimed at achieving (i.e., reducing gender essentialism). One possible solution to the problem is to discuss sexism—including sexism within the English language—with children. Bem (1983) suggested such a strategy in her classic paper on raising gender-aschematic children, but the effectiveness of such a strategy has not been studied. Future research should examine the consequences of providing children with a sexism schema (Bem, 1983) that includes the knowledge that words used to label individuals may come to shape our beliefs and expectations of them. Although the idea of combating so many subtle and pervasive forms of sexism may seem daunting, the fact that we can imagine alternatives gives us hope.

References

Akhtar, N., Carpenter, M., & Tomasello, M. (1996). The role of discourse novelty in early word learning. *Child Development*, **67**, 635–645.

American Psychological Assn Publication Manual Task Force (1977). Guidelines for nonsexist language in APA journals. *American Psychologist*, **32**, 487–494.

Bem, S. L. (1983). Gender schema theory and its implications for child development: Raising gender-aschematic children in a gender-schematic society. *Signs*, **8**, 598–616.

Bigler, R. S. (1995). The role of classification skill in moderating environmental influences on children's gender stereotyping: A study of the functional use of gender in the classroom. *Child Development*, **66**, 1072–1087.

Bigler, R. S., Brown, C. S., & Markell, M. (2001). When groups are not created equal: Effects of group status on the formation of intergroup attitudes in children. *Child Development*, **72**, 1151–1162.

Bohan, J. S. (1993). Regarding gender: Essentialism, constructionism, and feminist psychology. *Psychology of Women Quarterly*, **17**, 5–21.

Bradbard, M. R., Martin, C. L., Endsley, R. C., & Halverson, C. F. (1986). Influence of sex stereotypes on children's exploration and memory: A competence versus performance distinction. *Developmental Psychology*, **22**, 481–486.

Brauer, M., Wasel, W., & Niedenthal, P. (2000). Implicit and explicit components of prejudice. *Review of General Psychology*, **4**, 79–101.

Bussey, K., & Bandura, A. (1999). Social cognitive theory of gender development and differentiation. *Psychological Review*, **106**, 676–713.

Chodorow, N. (1978). *The reproduction of mothering: Psychoanalysis and the sociology of gender*. Berkeley, CA: University of California Press.

Coupland, N., Coupland, J., Giles, H., & Henwood, K. (1988). Accommodating the elderly: Invoking and extending a theory. *Language in Society*, **17**, 1–41.

Cunningham, W. A., Preacher, K. J., & Banaji, M. R. (2001). Implicit attitude measures: Consistency, stability, and convergent validity. *Psychological Science*, **12**, 163–170.

DeLoache, J. S., Cassidy, D. J., & Carpenter, C. J. (1987). The three bears are all boys: Mothers' gender labeling of neutral picture book characters. *Sex Roles*, **17**, 163–178.

Fazio, H. F., Jackson, J. R., Dunton, B. C., & Williams, C. J. (1995). Variability in automatic activation as an unobtrusive measure of racial attitudes: A bona fide pipeline? *Journal of Personality & Social Psychology*, **69**, 1013–1027.

Gelman, S. A. (2003). *The essential child: Origins of essentialism in everyday thought*. London: Oxford University Press.

Gentner, D., & Loewenstein, J. (2002). Relational language and relational thought. In E. Amsel & J. P. Byrnes (Eds.), *Language, literacy, and cognitive development: The development and consequences of symbolic communication* (pp. 87–120). Mahwah, NJ: Lawrence Erlbaum Associates, Publishers.

Graddol, D., & Swann, J. (1989). *Gender voices*. Oxford, UK: Basil Blackwell.

Henley, N. M. (1989). Molehill or mountain? What we know and don't know about sex bias in language. In M. Crawford & M. Gentry (Eds.), *Gender and thought: Psychological perspectives* (pp. 59–78). New York: Springer-Verlag.

Huttenlocher, J., Haight, W., Bryk, A., Seltzer, M., & Lyons, T. (1991). Early vocabulary growth: Relation to language input and gender. *Developmental Psychology*, **27**, 236–248.

Hyde, J. S. (1984). Children's understanding of sexist language. *Developmental Psychology*, **20**, 697–706.

Jacobson, M. B., & Insko, W. R. (1985). Use of nonsexist pronouns as a function of one's feminist orientation. *Sex Roles*, **13**, 1–7.

Killen, M., Pisacane, K., Lee-Kim, J., & Ardila-Rey, A. (2001). Fairness of stereotypes? Young children's priorities when evaluating group exclusion and inclusion. *Developmental Psychology*, **37**, 587–596.

Khorsroshahi, F. (1989). Penguins don't care, but women do: A social identity analysis of a Whorfian problem. *Language in Society*, **18**, 505–525.

Lambdin, J. R., Greer, K. M., Jibotian, K. S., Wood, K. R., & Hamilton, M. C. (2003). The animal = male hypothesis: Children's and adults' beliefs about the sex of non-sex-specific stuffed animals. *Sex Roles*, **48**, 471–482.

Leaper, C. (1994). Exploring the consequences of gender segregation on social relationships. In C. Leaper (Ed.), *Childhood gender segregation: Causes and consequences* (New Directions for Child Development, No. 65). San Francisco: Jossey-Bass.

Leaper, C. (1995a). Constructing representations of gender in the classroom [Review of *Gender identities and education: The impact of starting school*]. *American Journal of Psychology*, **108**, 300–304.

Leaper, C. (1995b). The use of "masculine" and "feminine" to describe women's and men's behavior. *Journal of Social Psychology*, **135**, 359–369.

Leaper, C. (2000). The social construction and socialization of gender during development. In P. H. Miller & E. K. Scholnick (Eds.), *Toward a feminist developmental psychology* (pp. 127–152). Florence, KY, US: Taylor & Francis/Routledge.

Leaper, C. (2002). Parenting girls and boys. In M. H. Bornstein (Ed.), *Handbook of parenting: Vol. 1: Children and parenting* (2nd ed., pp. 189–225). Mahwah, NJ: Lawrence Erlbaum Associates, Publishers.

Leaper, C., Anderson, K. J., & Sanders, P. (1998). Moderators of gender effects on parents' talk to their children: A meta-analysis. *Developmental Psychology*, **34**, 3–27.

Liben, L. S., & Bigler, R. S. (2002). The developmental course of gender differentiation: Conceptualizing, measuring, and evaluating constructs and pathways. *Monographs of the Society for Research in Child Development*, **67** (2), vii–147.

Liben, L. S., Bigler, R. S., & Krogh, H. R. (2002). Language at work: Children's gendered interpretations of occupational titles. *Child Development*, **73**, 810–828.

Lloyd, B., & Duveen, G. (1992). *Gender identities and education: The impact of starting school*. London: Harvester Wheatsheaf.

Lott, B. (1981). A feminist critique of androgyny: Toward the elimination of gender attributions for learned behavior. In C. Mayo & N. M. Henley (Eds.), *Gender and nonverbal behavior* (pp. 171–180). New York: Springer-Verlag.

Lytton, H., & Romney, D. M. (1991). Parents' differential socialization of boys and girls: A meta-analysis. *Psychological Bulletin*, **109**, 267–296.

Maccoby, E. E., & Jacklin, C. N. (1974). *The psychology of sex differences*. Stanford, CA: Stanford University Press.

MacKay, D. G. (1980). Psychology, prescriptive grammar, and the pronoun problem. *American Psychologist*, **35**, 444–449.

Marecek, J., & Hare-Mustin, R. T. (1991). A short history of the future: Feminism and clinical psychology. *Psychology of Women Quarterly*, **15**, 521–536.

Martin, C. L., Eisenbud, L., & Rose, H. (1995). Children's gender-based reasoning about toys. *Child Development*, **65**, 1453–1471.

Martin, C. L., & Ruble, D. (2004). Children's search for gender cues: Cognitive perspectives on gender development. *Current Directions in Psychological Science*, **13**, 67–70.

Martin, C. L., Ruble, D. N., & Szkrybalo, J. (2002). Cognitive theories of early gender development. *Psychological Bulletin*, **128**, 903–933.

Matheson, K., & Kristiansen, C. M. (1987). The effect of sexist attitudes and social structure on the use of sex-biased pronouns. *Journal of Social Psychology*, **127**, 395–398.

Perry, D. G., & Bussey, K. (1979). The social learning theory of sex differences: Imitation is alive and well. *Journal of Personality & Social Psychology*, **37**, 1699–1712.

Raasch, C., Leaper, C., & Bigler, R. (2004, April). *The influence of parental discussion on children's gender stereotyping*. Poster presented at the Gender Development Research Conference, San Francisco.

Rogoff, B. (1990). *Apprenticeship in thinking: Cognitive development in social context*. London: Oxford University Press.

Rosen, S., & Grandison, R. J. (1994). Effects of topic valence and pictorial distractor valence on verbalizing and evaluating topic-evoked visual imagery. *Motivation & Emotion*, **18**, 249–268.

Rubin, D. L., Greene, K., & Schncider, D. (1994). Adopting gender-inclusive language reforms: Diachronic and synchronic variation. *Journal of Language & Social Psychology*, **13**, 91–114.

Tenenbaum, H. R., & Leaper, C. (2002). Are parents' gender schemas related to their children's gender-related cognitions?: A meta analysis. *Developmental Psychology*, **38**, 615–630.

Acknowledgment

We thank Nameera Akhtar for comments on a draft of this manuscript.

CONTRIBUTORS

Susan A. Gelman (Ph.D., 1984, Stanford University) is the Frederick G. L. Huetwell Professor of Psychology at the University of Michigan. She is the author of *The Essential Child* (Oxford University Press, 2003). Her research focuses on early conceptual development and its relation to language.

Marianne G. Taylor (Ph.D., 1993, University of Michigan) is currently a lecturer in the Psychology Department at Pacific Lutheran University. Her research focuses on children's beliefs about gender and the role of parent–child conversations in the development of social understanding.

Simone P. Nguyen (Ph.D., 2003, University of Illinois, Champaign-Urbana) is an Assistant Professor in the Department of Psychology at the University of North Carolina at Wilmington. Her research focuses on conceptual development, particularly children's categories, inductive reasoning, and naive theories of biology.

Campbell Leaper (Ph.D., University of California Los Angeles, 1986) is Professor of Psychology at the University of California Santa Cruz. His work investigates the social construction and the socialization of gender and sexism. He has been especially interested in how contextual factors mediate and moderate gender typing. Also, much of his research has examined how language is used to define and maintain gender divisions. Other interests include gender-related variations in social identity, academic achievement, and awareness of sexism.

Rebecca S. Bigler (Ph.D., The Pennsylvania State University, 1991) is Associate Professor of Psychology at the University of Texas at Austin. Her work has concerned the development of gender and racial stereotypes, including how contextual factors serve to exaggerate or diminish their growth. She has also been active in developing and evaluating interventions designed to discourage the establishment and maintenance of gender and racial stereotypes.

STATEMENT OF EDITORIAL POLICY

The *Monographs* series is devoted to publishing developmental research that generates authoritative new findings and uses these to foster fresh, better integrated, or more coherent perspectives on major developmental issues, problems, and controversies. The significance of the work in extending developmental theory and contributing definitive empirical information in support of a major conceptual advance is the most critical editorial consideration. Along with advancing knowledge on specialized topics, the series aims to enhance cross-fertilization among developmental disciplines and developmental sub fields. Therefore, clarity of the links between the specific issues under study and questions relating to general developmental processes is important. These links, as well as the manuscript as a whole, must be as clear to the general reader as to the specialist. The selection of manuscripts for editorial consideration, and the shaping of manuscripts through reviews-and-revisions, are processes dedicated to actualizing these ideals as closely as possible.

Typically *Monographs* entail programmatic large-scale investigations; sets of programmatic interlocking studies; or—in some cases—smaller studies with highly definitive and theoretically significant empirical findings. Multi-authored sets of studies that center on the same underlying question can also be appropriate; a critical requirement here is that all studies address common issues, and that the contribution arising from the set as a whole be unique, substantial, and well integrated. The needs of integration preclude having individual chapters identified by individual authors. In general, irrespective of how it may be framed, any work that is judged to significantly extend developmental thinking will be taken under editorial consideration.

To be considered, submissions should meet the editorial goals of *Monographs* and should be no briefer than a minimum of 80 pages (including references and tables). There is an upper limit of 175–200 pages. In exceptional circumstances this upper limit may be modified. (Please submit four copies.) Because a *Monograph* is inevitable lengthy and usually sub-

144

stantively complex, it is particularly important that the text be well organized and written in clear, precise, and literate English. Note, however, that authors from non-English-speaking countries should not be put off by this stricture. In accordance with the general aims of SRCD, this series is actively interested in promoting international exchange of developmental research. Neither membership in the Society nor affiliation with the academic discipline of psychology are relevant in considering a *Monographs* submission.

The corresponding author for any manuscript must, in the submission letter, warrant that all coauthors are in agreement with the content of the manuscript. The corresponding author also is responsible for informing all coauthors, in a timely manner, of manuscript submission, editorial decisions, reviews received, and any revisions recommended. Before publication, the corresponding author also must warrant in the submission letter that the study has been conducted according to the ethical guidelines of the Society for Research in Child Development.

Potential authors who may be unsure whether the manuscript they are planning would make an appropriate submission are invited to draft an outline of what they propose, and send it to the Editor for assessment. This mechanism, as well as a more detailed description of all editorial policies, evaluation process, and format requirements can be found at the Editorial Office web site (http://astro.temple.edu/-overton/monosrcd.html) or by contacting the Editor, Wills F. Overton, Temple University-Psychology, 1701 North 13th St. – Rm 567, Philadelphia, PA 19122-6085 (e-mail: monosrcd@temple.edu) (telephone: 1-215-204-7360).

Monographs of the Society for Reasearch in Child Development (ISSN 0037-976X), one of two publications of Society of Research in Child Development, is published three times a year by Blackwell Publishing, Inc., with offices at 350 Main Street, Malden, MA 02148, USA, and 9600 Garsington Road, Oxford OX4 2XG, UK. Call US (800) 835-6770 or (781) 388-8206, UK +44 (0) 1865 778315; fax US (781) 388-8232, UK +44 (0) 1865 471775; e-mail US subscrip@bos.blackwellpublishing.com, UK customerservices@oxon.blackwellpublishing. com. A subscription to *Monographs of the SRCD* comes with a subscription to *Child Development* (published bimonthly).

INFORMATION FOR SUBSCRIBERS   For new orders, renewals, sample copy requests, claims, change of address, and all other subscription correspondence, please contact the Journals Subscription Department at your nearest Blackwell office.

INSTITUTIONAL PREMIUM RATES* FOR MONOGRAPHS OF THE SRCD/CHILD DEVELOPMENT 2004   The Americas $420, Rest of World £298. Customers in Canada should add 7% GST to The Americas price or provide evidence of entitlement to exemption. Customers in the UK and EU should add VAT at 5% or provide a VAT registration number or evidence of entitlement to exemption.

*Includes print plus premium online access to the current and all available backfiles. Print and online-only rates are also available. For more information about Blackwell Publishing journals, including online access information, terms and conditions, and other pricing options, please visit www.blackwellpublishing.com or contact our customer service department, tel: (800) 835-6770 or (781) 388-8206 (US office); +44 (0)1865 778315 (UK office).

BACK ISSUES   Back issues are available from the publisher at the current single issue rate.

MICROFORM   The journal is available on microfilm. For microfilm service, address inquiries to ProQuest Information and Learning, 300 North Zeeb Road, Ann Arbor, MI 48106-1346, USA. Bell and Howell Serials Customer Service Department: (800) 521-0600 × 2873.

ADVERTISING   For information and rates, please visit the journal's website at www.blackwellpublishing.com/MONO email: blackwellads@aidcvt.com, or contact Faith Elliott, Blackwell Advertising Representative, 50 Winter Sport Lane, PO Box 80, Williston, VT 05495. Phone: 800-866-1684 or Fax: 802-864-7749.

MAILING   Journal is mailed Standard Rate. Mailing to rest of world by Deutsche Post Global Mail. Canadian mail is sent by Canadian publications mail agreement number 40573520. Postmaster: Send all address changes to Monographs of the Societey for Research in Child Development, Blackwell Publishing Inc., Journals Subscription Department, 350 Main St., Malden, MA 02148-5018.

 Sign up to receive Blackwell *Synergy* free e-mail alerts with complete *Monographs of the SRCD* tables of contents and quick links to article abstracts from the most current issue. Simply go to www.blackwell-synergy.com, select the journal from the list of journals, and click on "Sign-up" for FREE email table of contents alerts.